Michael Jackson

The Inspirational Life Story of Michael Jackson

(The Truth Behind the King of Pop's Adventurous Life Journey)

Nelle Williamson

Published By **Regina Loviusher**

Nelle Williamson

All Rights Reserved

Michael Jackson: The Inspirational Life Story of Michael Jackson (The Truth Behind the King of Pop's Adventurous Life Journey)

ISBN 978-1-77485-878-3

No part of this guidebook shall be reproduced in any form without permission in writing from the publisher except in the case of brief quotations embodied in critical articles or reviews.

Legal & Disclaimer

The information contained in this ebook is not designed to replace or take the place of any form of medicine or professional medical advice. The information in this ebook has been provided for educational & entertainment purposes only.

The information contained in this book has been compiled from sources deemed reliable, and it is accurate to the best of the Author's knowledge; however, the Author cannot guarantee its accuracy and validity and cannot be held liable for any errors or omissions. Changes are periodically made to this book. You must consult your doctor or get professional medical advice before using any of the suggested remedies, techniques, or information in this book.

Upon using the information contained in this book, you agree to hold harmless the Author from and against any damages, costs, and expenses, including any legal fees potentially resulting from the application of any of the information provided by this guide. This disclaimer applies to any damages or injury caused by the use and application, whether directly or indirectly, of any advice or information presented, whether for breach of contract, tort, negligence, personal injury, criminal intent, or under any other cause of action.

You agree to accept all risks of using the information presented inside this book. You need to consult a professional medical practitioner in order to ensure you are both able and healthy enough to participate in this program.

TABLE OF CONTENTS

Chapter 1: Magic Iconic Imagery.............. 1

Chapter 2: Analyze, Extract, Reinvent 13

Chapter 3: Goal-Setting"Wishing" - Affirmed... 29

Chapter 4: Abandon To The Creative Powers - Descover, Do Not Create 44

Chapter 5: Workethic Of A Perfectionist 56

Chapter 6: Rise Across The Hate 74

Chapter 7: Mystique Metamorphosis 91

Chapter 8: Career................................. 105

Chapter 9: "Death" 153

Chapter 1: Magic Iconic Imagery

"They simply want amazing experiences, they'd like to escape. We'd like to take them to places that they've not been to before."

What makes a star an international star? What makes their status from inquisitive to extraordinary? The answer lies in famous imagery and the capability to incite wonder, awe and awe through a look or a look. The greats all have it, be it their hairstyle, clothing or gesture, dance movement, or the cover of their album.

Iconic imagery is all about creating an image that draws attention and provokes thought. It should also in the event that it is possible, makes us in awe. The most important thing is to instantly be recognized as being theirs. The Beatles have their "Mop Tops' Marilyn Monroe had her white dress while Elvis Presley had his glittering caped jumpsuit. Looking to become the biggestand most iconic star of all, Michael began to create an appearance and style that could rival his idols. The secret to his success? Create a magical environment.

It's the Motown 25 Performance

In one magical night in 1983, Michael would present to the world not just one but four unforgettable pictures: The hat the glove, the moonwalk as well as the freeze of toes. However, it was the only show on TV that Michael was not interested in doing.

His previous label, Motown Records, founded in 1959, had made the decision to commemorate their 25th anniversary a year before the official date. It was as if the universe had conspired to bring about the occasion with the release of Michael's 1983 single "Billie Jean,"" his most well-known track. It took some convincing, since Michael was adamant about live television performances. At the age of 24 Michael was working to promote his newly released album Thriller and was trying to become the world's most famous star. A major part of his strategy was to be in complete control of every aspect of his appearance. He wanted people to only see what the image he wanted to be able to see. Through the music video (which were called short films) they could select every angle, each shot, and create an experience that met his highest standards. Television was too volatile and the quality could not be assured. He straight-facedly said to Motown "no."

Michael was just finishing shooting the revolutionary documentary Beat It, and as the fate of things the editing was taking place at Motown Studios in Los Angeles. The President of Motown Records, Berry Gordy, (the man responsible for the Jackson Five's worldwide popularity,) heard that Michael was present in the studio, and came to meet Michael. After a lengthy discussion, Michael accepted the show. The only condition was that was that of including the song that is not Motown "Billie Jean." Gordy joyfully agreed.

On the 16th of May on the night of the show's broadcast America was already in awe of the new appearance of Michael Jackson. His album Thriller was dominating at the top of the charts and two short movies Billie Jean and Beat It were awe-inspiring to the masses. Then, they'd get the chance to see the artist live on television.

Michael appeared on the stage with his brothers wearing a sequin-sewn black jacket over a silver sequined shirt. While he sparkled in the spotlight the audience noticed something was different. He was wearing only one glove. Before they could ask why, the music started. Michael as well as his siblings dazzled audiences with a selection of their previous songs, but the main performance was to be yet. After saying goodbye to his brothers from on stage Michael was moving around, smiling in a playful manner. He appeared like someone with an unexpected gift to share with the world.

"Those were magical moments with all my brothers including Jermaine. However, as it's true that those were great songs."

Michael smiled as the crowd sensed there was a possibility of something happening.

"But particularly, I love... some of the new tunes." 3

And then the hit song "Billie Jean" started. Michael pulled the black fedora hat off the floor, and pulled it up onto his head. It was half-covered with his face. Michael stood up with the left foot pointing towards the front, revealing the sparkling socks were on him. After an stomp and turn, Michael threw his hat towards the other side. America was not watching a live show on television and instead was witnessing an iconic and significant event in pop culture history. Michael was dancing and spinning as he swung at the sky using his white glove then he performed to the world with an unforgettable show-stopper: the moonwalk.

As Michael moved backwards the audience could hear gasps from the crowd. There was no one who had seen an artist move this fast. Michael completed the moonwalk, flipped three times before landing on his feet. Michael had presented the world with four amazing iconic images which was when the mythology of Michael Jackson created. From that point his life, as well as the world of music forever be different.

Let's take a closer look at the famous images of the night, along with Michael's other stunning images.

The Sequined Glove

If he'd worn 2 gloves, his results could not have been exactly identical. There was something about using just one glove that set the imagination of the entire world to ablaze.

Only one glove is on. Was the second glove? Who is the only person who wears one glove?

Michael did something that every iconic image is characterized by... distinctiveness. Since nobody else was able to only wear just one pair of gloves, the glove became his. Why did he put on the glove?

Michael utilized the one white glove when he employs his white gloves, in order to attract attention to the elegant movements of his hands and also to create misdirection. Michael wanted his audience to be amazed by each motion of his body which is why he needed to disengage the audience from focusing on the person's face. The factor it was sequins made it easier for him to accomplish this. Michael realized that people's eyes immediately follow light as well, and with a stunning glove, he was able to draw the attention of those around him to where the focus was. If Michael had performed "Billie Jean" without the glove or the sparkling socks, the audience might not have seen the beauty of the performance. Michael was focused on demonstrating the beauty of dancing. He wasn't a performer however, but rather an unstoppable juggernaut of fun from head to the toe.

Off the stage, the glove assumed an ethereal appearance when Michael was struck by third-degree burns to his head during the shooting of an Pepsi commercial during January 1984. After being transported into the medical facility, Michael was informed that there were numerous news crews waiting outside, eager for an opportunity to film. The opportunity to get publicity and publicity, he made only one demand: "Bring me my glove." On an ambulance, his head wrapped in the blanket covering about two-thirds of his body, the sparkling glove emerged from his blanket and waved to the world, hoping to be assured that he would be okay. The glove was transformed into the man. It was the man, and its graceful motion signaled that he was well. This is the most iconic image that is impressive.

There is the Moonwalk as well as Toe Freeze

The illusion of walking backwards when you appear to walk in the direction of forwards is an illusion. visually appealing which will make the viewer want to know the method and then watch it over and over again. This is the essence of any fantastic illusion. It's obvious but you aren't sure how to interpret it and you wish you could have it done yourself. Music journalist Robert Hilburn, who was in the audience on that night, actually contacted Michael's publicist following day to inquire whether Michael used an escalator while performing! That's what Michael wanted to achieve. It was so stunning that it was beyond human capabilities that an Hollywood special effects crew must be involved.

The white socks with glitter created a dazzling illusion as if they were a source of magic force that could make the move happen. As with the white gloves the socks drew attention. After Michael was done with his moonwalk, the actor whirled three times before landing on his feet, suspended in motion, even if just for a moment. The movement is about challenging the limits of physics, which adds to the'mystical mysterious nature of his persona and, being so distinctive that it became his signature as he utilized an illustration of the toe freeze to create his "MJJ Productions" logo.

It's the Fedora Hat and the Smooth Criminal Lean

The concept is to put on a cap, something interesting and sinister that would create excitement and intrigue. The hat functioned as a glove. In the hat covering one's face Michael put the focus on his entire body. In Motown 25 Michael was only wearing the hat to introduce the track. For the film Smooth Criminal, however, the hat was utilized to its maximum benefit. The gangster of the 1930s was a glamor as he took the audience on a journey into an enigma filled with intrigue and danger. Smooth Criminal is regarded by many as Michael's finest dance video. A large part of the reason for this is because Michael kept his face hidden throughout the dance, forcing viewers to watch his body.

There's a pause in the song. the lights go out, and the dancers huddle together. Michael removes his hat like he is attempting to summon the force of music to come back. With a shout of "Annie is you alright?" he snaps his hat back on with the music and the lights. Michael is connecting the power of his cap to the music. The hat serves as a signal for the crowd; once it's on , the music plays and Michael is able to achieve the impossible. After giving a grin at a girl who is who was watching from the out the window, Michael pushes the hat upwards and covers his face completely and executing another iconic dance routine: the lean. Michael is able to lean forward at 45 degrees and then defies gravity for a moment, and then returns back to the normal place. The hat and lean are interspersed. Michael has never done the illusion without a mask over his face. He incorporated the hat into magical powers within the mind of the audience, either conscious or not. The result? The audience credits magic powers to the hat. As a magician's wand which isn't really a weapon, Michael transformed the piece of clothing into a magical item that enabled him to accomplish the impossible.

The Thriller Jacket

Of all the elaborate Michael's costumes throughout his career, none had the impact as powerful as his Thriller Jacket. It was auctioned during June of 2011 $1.8 million, an buyer called the jacket "the most valuable piece of rock and roll memorabilia from the past." The jacket was created for the first time by Deborah Landis, the wife of the film's director, John Landis, the jacket is able to achieve what many of Michael's costumes have done create a contrast between him and his surroundings.

When Michael dances with the band of ghouls, the vivid blood-red hue stands out against the gray, dark tones of the dead. Blood symbolizes the spirit of life. Michael is the force that lives in this short movie. Michael's vitality enables him to conquer the dead and defeat the dangers they pose to us by making them dance with him, and become the subjects to his pure power. The result is hypnotic and showcases Michael's mystical power once more.

Debrah Landis wore an black V on the jacket to enhance Michael's feeling of control. "It's geometric and structural and I was looking for an appealing shape. The V of the jacket really mirrors the pyramidal form of the choreography. He's at the top of the chevron and they're moving toward the spectator." 4.

The Leçon of his Secret

Make your style more than just beautiful; make it magical. If someone can make others believe that they're in a different world or have powers that are beyond the ordinary person They will gain recognition. Similar to the magician with his wand, a face must be energised by making it appear as if it can facilitate something extraordinary. Michael's amazing gloves and socks helped him perform his moonwalk and frozen toe, the fedora hat enabled Michael to defy gravity while the Thriller jacket let him take control of the undead. Incredibly iconic images, combined with magic, can trigger an overwhelming public reaction.

*****

Chapter 2: Analyze, Extract, Reinvent

"The most effective education around is watching masters in action." 5

Michael Jackson is known as an extraordinary dancer, singer and songwriter, however, few people are aware that his analytical abilities were among his best qualities. He was a keen observer and always kept his eyes open, looking at the surroundings, taking ideas, reimagining the ideas, refining them and then repackaging them in his MJ style of magic. Quincy Jones described his mind as"a "laser beam." Elizabeth Taylor said he was similar to "litmus paper,"" as well Celine Dion simply described him as "a genius." To comprehend how he became successful it is essential to understand the way his mind worked.

Study the Top

When Michael was touring with his brothers during the 1960s, playing in concert halls alongside other performers and was exposed to some of the top entertainers of the time and the pioneers of the contemporary pop sound. Following they performed, the Jackson Five would perform, as his brothers were sitting backstage and chatting with their friends, young Michael was often found behind the stage, beneath an old curtain that was dusty, in silence, watching other performers perform. As Michael put it,

"I was able to watch every step, every movement each turn, twist and every grind or scream, every emotion, and every slight movement. It was my education, and also my entertainment." 5

Michael was immersed in the art and observing what made the audience excited, as well as looking for strategies to boost his performance. Berry Gordy recalled, "He was a consummate student. he studied the best performers and later became the best." 6 However, it was not just other performers Michael sat and watched. Michael was always prepared to draw ideas from whatever that he observed, and sometimes even from the most unexpected of places.

Be a People Observer

One of the best aspects of Michael's life is the fact that a lot of his followers met him without even realizing that they were doing it. Michael was known to wear disguises or amazing disguises, and travel to research the world around his. He could be found in the music store, in an eatery, an intersection or even knocking on your door to distribute Watchtower magazines. He wanted to know the real-life reactions of people when they perceived him as a non-entity instead of a star. You might have watched the "Captain Eo" 3D movie at Disneyland and then walked right by him.

"I'd be sitting on a bench at Disneyland and dream of. I'd be there for a while and I'll never forget, I was awed by it. I learned so muchfrom looking at people, analyzing their personality. This is what I love about." 7

Michael was always focused on his customers. The more he realized that he was aware of what was happening around him, better his ability to provide what people wanted.

"One time , I was in the record store, completely disguised, these women were grabbing my album, and talking about me. I was actually right in front of them. It was fantastic. I absolutely loved it." 8

However, Michael did not just go to amusement parks or shopping malls disguised, he was in the slums around the world. He wanted to know how everyone lives, not just those living in Hollywood. When Michael directed his short movie Beat It in Los Angeles's homeless area Skid Row, his co-stars were stunned when Michael confessed that he'd been there before, in the dark, by himself. Michael utilized his experiences to create songs like "They Don't care" as well as "Why You Wanna Trip On Me." When Michael sang about destruction and poverty this was because the experience was first-hand for him.

Keep Your Fingers on the Pulse

Michael was always looking to be doing things that were fresh and innovative. Alongside studying the greatest, he also was also interested in the present. He was determined to stay current and competitive. In order to achieve this the need to analyse his competitors. Each week the compilation tapes were created by his team, and handed over to Michael to take in and study. These were among the top 10 charts in all genres. Michael would take his time listening to them in order to determine what the trends were to take it before the rest of us would. Michael scrutinized every aspect of each song, pointing out its flaws as well as its strengths and, most importantly, its potential. He would separate each sound that came into his head, and then examine every instrument used in the song. A bad song could contain an incredible beat, or a fascinating guitar break, or interesting lyrics. He was shaping his song-creating mind and stock piling up his collection of musical sounds.

"I love to collect sounds and place them under the microscope and talk about how we can modify the sound's character." 9

Michael's curiosity about the world was not only restricted to music. He was interested in what was available in book stores and what the public was watching at the cinema. If he could figure out what people were interested in, and what was the reason they were interested then he could make music and dance that excite people.

Mold Your Voice

Michael's voice isn't only an amazing story of being blessed however, it is it is also one of analysis and growth. As Michael demonstrated with his rendition of Smokey's smash hit song "Who's Loving You" on the Ed Sullivan Show at age 12 years old, Michael had the most soulful voice anyone had ever heard. Michael was the most impressive by delivering emotions of love, pain anger, angst, and sadness. However, Michael's voice as an adult wasn't the adult version of his youthful self. It was a voice was formed and developed by watching his idols.

Diana Ross is known for her role in introducing The Jackson Five to the world However, not many people know that, as a young boy, Michael lived with Diana Ross. When the family relocated into Los Angeles upon signing with Motown Records, they were divided between Berry Gordy and Diana Ross who resided at the exact same address located in Beverly Hills. Michael was her protégé and he was taught to imitate her sweet voice. The oohs she sang with her signature were imitated by Michael and resurfaced in a variety of his songs. In the album he released in 2001, Invincible her delicate way of singing is heard on his magnificent track "Speechless."

As he got older in his voice, his range grew from boy soprano up to high tenor and, despite influences from vocalists such as Diana the voice of his assumed a gender-neutral quality. His performance in the choir of "We are the world" in 1985 demonstrated the ability he had developed his voice to showcase female and male shades. In contrast to his childhood voice that echoed his idols Michael's adult voice was unique. Michael was able to create his own distinctive vocal voices you've ever heard.

Michael also borrowed his inspiration from Mavis Staples who was the lead singer of the 1960s group The Staples Singers, incorporating her signature "Shamone" along with "lay it down on my" into his brilliant R & B song, "Bad."

"I'm Bad! I'm Bad! Shamone!" 10

Mavis discovered the re-incorporation of her style after the mother of her child called to inform her that Michael stole her words. However, Mavis was elated. "It's an entirely new word that I came up with! Instead of saying 'Come on! and tell me what you think, I used "SHA-mone. It's like trying to appear smooth. He was able to pick to it. It made me feel great." 11

Following the huge popularity with Thriller as well as Bad Michael's voice continued to develop Some would say because of the need to express his frustration and anger at the world surrounding him. To convey these feelings, Michael added some real rock hues in his vocals. "Jam," "Why You Want to Trip on Me," "D.S.," "We've Had Enough," "Shout," and "Morphine" show how his voice can express emotion without having to know the lyrics. It's part of his international appeal. The listeners don't require a translation of the lyrics, they sense the meaning Michael conveys.

Get ready to dance Like the Best

James Brown, without a doubt was Michael's very first idol in dance. Before Brown there were dancers and singing, however this guy mixed the two and gave the viewers a visual and a vocal performance. Brown established the way for the young Michael to pursue, using amazing twists and turns. And at the age of ten, Michael could already dance at a level comparable to his. However, wanting to be more than the best, Michael cast his eyes farther than Motown and fixed his eyes all on the legendary Fred Astaire.

Fred Astaire, a Broadway showman who brought his talent to the screen during the 1930s was considered to be the most skilled dancer of all time. Astaire created the art of dance, and his work became the basis for several of Michael's short film. People who are familiar with the art will recognize his movements in a variety of Michael's shows. The violent dance routine featured in the film Black or White left many in the year 1991 thinking they were crazy and wondering if it was an actual recreation of a scene in the movie The Sky's The Limit, where Astaire smashes down the bar and dances on the bar's top then kicks beer bottle all before throwing the bar stool at the champagne glasses in a tower smashing them, and also the mirror behind during the process.

Astaire's influence can be observed in other MJ performances. The massive silhouette projections Michael utilized in his live performances in "Smooth Criminal" were first glimpsed in Astaire's Swing Time. The dances that took place on the ceiling and walls of the spaceship in Scream were very like Astaire's gravity-defying routine from Royal Wedding. Michael was awed by these amazing scenes, and recreated the same for a contemporary audience. This is why a lot of Michael's followers, learning of his admiration in Fred Astaire, are now exploring these amazing films that were made more than 100 years back.

The most significant gift Astaire presented Michael his film The Band Wagon, for without it there wouldn't be the cult short film Smooth Criminal. Michael's masterpiece, which is viewed by many as surpassing that of the Thriller the short, basically his film, set to Michael's energetic track. The Band Wagon is

The Band Wagon, Astaire is a sexy and mysterious figure in his gangster outfit of the 1930s and gangster attire, dances in a saloon surrounded by beautiful women, while fighting off other Gangsters. The choreography that was used to create the scene in Smooth Criminal was lifted directly and there was no need to alter it. However, in Michael's reimagined version, the dance set is larger and the dance is more edgy and the look is unique. Michael's inclusion of the lean takes Smooth Criminal on top of the list. If you're trying to duplicate an amazing artwork Michael's idea is to create it larger and more impressive.

In all his influences in his life, ranging starting with James Brown to Charlie Chaplin to Diana Ross, perhaps Michael was most grateful to Astaire in the form of dedicating his autobiography from 1988 Moonwalk to Astaire. It was a sentiment that was felt by all and felt by Astaire, since Astaire declared the following: Michael was "the most famous dancer of the century." and shortly before dying in the year 1987, he stated, "I didn't want to go on without knowing who my descendant was. Thank you, Michael!"

Michael's dream of becoming the best dancer on the planet led him to spread his net all the way. He would travel through the streets of the 1980s, trying for the amazing break dancers, so that they could be watched in motion. He attributes the moonwalk to street dancers, and says that the moonwalk was his invention "refined" the moonwalk. Spielberg dinosaurs also served as an opportunity to test new movements. After watching the Tyrannosaurus Rex in the 1993 hit film Jurassic Park, Michael incorporated the head move into his stage show "Billie Jean." It's not surprising that Michael would take a look at a dinosaur and then interpret it as an dance routine? However, animals were always in his mind to help him come up with ideas.

"He would listen to tapes of gazelles, cheetahs, and panthers in order to emulate the natural elegance of their movements," stated Quincy Jones in his autobiography. 12 In fact, Michael's dancing was a manifestation of all the individuals and events he seen and believed worthy to be shared.

The development of his style in his Thriller and Bad time saw the introduction to add the "POW!" to his dance moves. Michael loved Bruce Lee's movements, especially the incredible display of strength that Lee applied to his kicks and punches. Lee would get his muscles tight upon contact, resulting in an explosive force explosion that broke through the air. Michael's dance moves were initially soft and fluid, transformed into an impressive tour de force. In the video Jam, Michael attempts to instruct his co-star, Michael Jordan, how to dance. Michael tells the legend of basketball to pour all his effort into the movements. "POW!" "BOOM!" He yells, demonstrating to the awkward Jordan how to perform the move.

"Feel all the energy that is coming from your palm." 13

One legend One legend, learning from another.

Imagine a Child as a Child
Michael was never a fan of those who told him to "grow to be a grown-up," because he

believed that only through the eyes of children could he experience the world, gain through it and develop.

"The child's innocence is for me the source of endless imagination. This is the potential of each person." 14

For him, children were the most beautiful, and he wished to emulate the same mindset.
"They have amazing, brilliant stages and then, when they reach older and lose their innocence, they go through a period of. Many people believe that certain things are childlike however, they are actually just kids who've lost the true magic because they've stopped looking and sifting and finding out. I am convinced of that." 15

Michael was always amazed by the way a child will look around the surroundings, examining every inch, looking at what adults can't observe because of the "conditioning." Although he was an entrepreneur with a million dollars and having traveled around the world, he battled for his life against getting bored constantly trying to perceive things as if it was the first time as a child would. The childlike side of him was evident during the photo shoot for the Thriller album's cover. Unsatisfied with the outfits available, Michael's gaze at photographer David Zimmerman's white suit and he asked to wear it instead. Zimmerman removed himself from his suit, and loaned it to Michael and then the famous album cover was designed.

The Leçon of his Secret

Michael was a student of the greatest and , like a reverse engineer who disassembles a piece of machinery to find out how it functions, Michael deconstructed the greats and laid the entire pieces in front of him and set about to build something larger and more efficient. He observed the things that was working, and what did not work, which ideas could be borrowed and how to improve upon. By taking these pieces then adding his unique personal touch and a unique style, he made the star. Don't be enthralled by the greatest, take a break and break up what they accomplished and then see how the pieces are put together.

As Michael Do your best to look at everything for the first time similar to a newborn and you'll be amazed by things that you do not observe due to your maturing. From what you see, take a close look and break it down and let them be the basis for something else. Perhaps an intriguing book cover might inspire an entirely new story, or an overheard conversation in the subway would provide a fantastic basis for an upcoming song. Think about everything and ask yourself and think about how I can make use of this?

Review other's work and think about what if you could do with it. What if they'd taken this approach instead? What if you had changed this or added this? You might watch a film and conclude that it's okay, but think about the ways it could have been better and then note it down. It is training your brain to function as Michael's did. Study everything, take ideas, and then rethink Michael's method of success.

*****

Chapter 3: Goal-Setting "Wishing" - Affirmed

"Go to the next level Follow your dreams, pursue your ideals. You can be everything you'd like to be. You can become an astronaut, scientist, a top doctor, and of course, be the best art therapist." 16

The most remarkable thing of Michael's existence and one that is not widely recognized one, is that he did not fall in the trap that children are prone to fall into the kind of person who believes that they've done everything they could and that they've done their bestand they'll never look or act like they did. Michael did indeed reach the top of his game as a young man, making the transition from working-class Gary, Indiana, to glamorous Beverly Hills, having a series of hits that reached the top of the charts and traveling around the world as a celebrity. Many would have been content to leave and be proud of having put in their best effort, and let newer artists fill the void and enjoy the millions they have earned through years of dedication; But not Michael. Jackson Five's success was a disappointment. Jackson Five's success has left Michael's dream of a lifetime not fulfilled, as Michael always had aspired to becoming the most impressive showman among all.

Write and declare your wishes

Wishing is a concept that is believed to be an innocent game, or maybe a snarky expression. I would love to be wealthy or could be rich. To Michael Wishing was more than a mere thought. It was the real belief in the power of magic. Michael was convinced that wishing worked and given his successes who would argue with his belief?

As a child, prior to when diving into the water He would extend his arms upwards, extending them up to the sky as if he were sending wish to God. I would like to own the most-seller album ever. He would make his wish known and then plunge into the ocean. Michael didn't believe that dreams should be kept within one's heart and that they should be made available, in order to bring them real. Michael employed a variety of methods to make his dreams fly.

"I believe in the power of wishes and the ability of a person to bring a dream real. I do. Every time I saw the setting sun, I'd dream of my secret wishes just before the sun was tucked beneath the western horizon before disappearing. It appeared like the sun removed my wish. I'd get it right before the last speck of light went away. A wish isn't just a desire It's a plan. It's something that your conscious and subconscious mind can aid in making a reality." 5

Michael invented a world in which wishes could be granted anytime. There were wishing fountains built in his homes. In Neverland there was his "wishing tree,"" which was a tree that can be climbable with a deck that was perched in the branches to relax and gaze at the night sky. It was possible to find him in the tree in awe, waiting patiently for the shooting star to shine across the dark night and his wishes could be carried to the realm where it would be a reality.

Do your best to be the best
The album of 1979 Off The Wall was a huge success. It was the highest-selling single by an

artist solo selling ten million copies as well as four top-ten hits, and securing the Grammy Award. However, Michael was not thrilled. According to him, it should have been sold at least twice as much. The top ten songs ought to have all been top ten with there was only one Grammy? It was a disgrace to Michael. Michael did not even attend the ceremony, feeling let down because his album wasn't selected for the 'Album of the Year. Michael said"to himself, "I'll showcase them" and set to work on the album which was going to be Thriller.

The year 1982 was a time of the economy in recession, and with more than 10% unemployment, record sales dropped. The notion that Michael could replicate the success Off The Wall Off The Wall was seen as a long-shot and his label was blunt in telling the singer that it was not possible. Michael responded, with all sincerity in all sincerity, that Thriller was going to be the most successful album ever. They laughed right at him. But this was a dream Michael was pursuing ever since the age of a child and he believed that the stars had aligned for him to finally shine.

Michael and Quincy were a team of hard-working, often 24-hour work days working to their limit. The effort paid off the album that Michael had imagined came to fruition. The album became the top-selling album ever, spending over a staggering thirty-seven weeks in the top of the charts and is currently selling more than 100 million copies. To those who had worked with Michael his success, it took the audience by shock. However, to Michael the success was simply his dream, and even goal which was realized exactly in the way he had planned.

Set Goals Extraordinary
If you don't set your sights high, you'll not be able to reach your potential. Michael believed in this and set what appeared to be often impossible and unrealistic goals. The album released in 1987 Bad was designed to surpass Thriller however it failed to achieve. However, Michael's lofty goals allowed him to surpass Thriller in a different way, since Bad recorded five US top-ten albums, something no previous album had ever managed to do. Michael realized that if you set your sights for the top, even if you aren't successful trying to

achieve the highest ensures that you can achieve remarkable feats regardless.

Michael was averse to mediocrity, as well as people who sold themselves short and, more importantly, would tell him how far he was able to go. He was taught that you should do all you have, and always strive to be the top. Never compromise; always strive to be the best.

"Even when you're cleaning the floors, or painting your ceiling, you'll do it better than everyone else anywhere else regardless of what it is you're doing." 17

The Jackson children were taught the phrase "Think it, feel it, believe itand and make it happen." The 18-year old Michael was a firm believer in this. Thinking about goals, planning the route and executing the plan was an everyday occurrence. Once he committed his thoughts on it, he became unstoppable. With blinders on Michael would begin into action.

Visualize the goal

Michael believed his dreams were achievable because he could feel them in his mind. He would often write down his goals and then pinned them on mirrors, walls or furniture. For Thriller He added "100 million" upon the wall in the mirror in his Encino home. He viewed it every day and said it would come true. I'll make it happen. The reason he did this was so his goals could confront him his goals, and was forced to act what the goals had instructed him to do. Pining goals to the walls is about granting the authority to your goals to let them rule your actions. The goals of his masters were his own and he was their loyal and faithful servant.

To show a more visual representation of his dreams, Michael created vivid dream books. The dream books were the place where he wrote down everything wishes he wanted to become a reality, sketched images and pasted cut-outs cut from newspapers and magazines. Before he invented Neverland it was all inside his book of dreams. There were images of elephants, rides children playing and stars shooting. He would gaze at these pictures and allow them to sink into his brain. Once you have a goal in mind the goal is set and all you need to do is to get to work. Michael loved the tale of the sculptor's story and his work. People inquire about how he makes such beautiful shapes, and Michael says, "It was already there and I only disclosed it." Michael saw the works of art in his head and believed that they were already there and began work on creating them.

Meditate

In addition to making picture books about his desires, Michael took meditation very serious. He would dedicate 50 minutes of meditation and clear his mind, and focussing on his goals. He would select a calm location, perhaps with the gentle thumping of water to calm him. He would then think about all the things he desired. Michael would think about it for so long that he believed that the goals he wanted were already there. Whatever he desired, Michael would make it clear to himself over and over and burying his goals in his mind. He would repeat this process continuously for twenty five minutes, then take a break for another twenty-five minutes. The rest was equally important as his meditation, as he wanted the goals he set out to establish and grow on themselves. Michael was actually creating his mind as an engine for creativity.

Place your order and receive

Since Michael was able to program his brain to become an engine of creativity He was delighted when the thing he requested was delivered. His huge hit "Billie Jean" was the result of a request. He told himself the song he was writing should have one with an incredible bass line. He put the seed in the ground and let his dream develop. The next day the bass line was revealed to him. He was so fascinated by the tune that he was listening to in his mind that he didn't realize that the car in which he was was on fire. The driver stopped the car and as they waited to get assistance, Michael was nearly oblivious to the possibility that he might have perished. "Billie Jean" was on the radio and, like millions who were soon to be amazed, Michael also was in total shock and in stunned.

The 80s anthem "We are the World" was also an envelope that was sent to you. Quincy Jones asked Michael to compose a song for the "USA for Africa project. It was one that would resonate with people, bring them closer and motivate the people to change their lives. The order was made. Michael got up the next day to the tune that was playing through his mind. If you ask for it, you will receive it.

Make Positive Affirmations

Michael was fond of recording his positive thoughts on cassette and replay them to himself throughout the day.

"You have confidence... you're solid... you're gorgeous... you're the best." 18

It was meant to eliminate those who doubted, the ones who swore at him and push forward to new heights. Michael was familiar with the ways Muhammad Ali, who declared to the world that he was the best and most powerful, could pull off astonishing victories repeatedly even when the odds were against his success. The power of self-belief was there. Ali defeated the stronger and younger George Foreman in the famed Rumble in the

Jungle, a testimony to affirmations that are positive.

While not wanting to appear proud, Michael would never state his accomplishments in public like Ali did. Do you think of the quiet Michael holding an event to proclaim that he was the greatest? This wasn't Michael's style therefore the tape recorder was the tool he used to program his mind to achieve.

Be Confident in Yourself

In an interview with USA Today in 2001 about whether he was still doubting his worth after the shaky sales of Invincible the film, he said,

"Never. I am confident in my capabilities. I'm a true believer. I will never be stopped if I set my mind to it."

He saw beyond the temporary, knowing his recordings would be listened to and selling for a hundred years.

"Invincible is a huge success. The moment The Nutcracker Suite was first presented in the public eye, it absolutely failed. The most important thing is the ending of the story." [19]

The Nutcracker Suite is a Russian ballet that was composed by the composer Pyotr Illyich Tchaikovsky. It was not a success upon its debut in 1892. The music was amazing it was enchantingly haunting that it's popularity only seemed to expand and increase. In the more than one hundred years after its debut, The Nutcracker Suite still amazes listeners.

In reality, the album of Tchaikovsky was Michael's standard because every song is a masterpiece with no "album tracks" as well as "fillers." Michael would remind the musicians who he worked together in studios that they, too, as Tchaikovsky composed music that could be played for many years to in the future.

"Great songs and music will never die. The fashions change, culture changes fashions, and customs but great music remains in the same place. We continue to listen to Mozart in the present; Tchaikovsky, Rachmaninov, any of of the greatest composers. Music that is great is like a wonderful sculpture, the best painting. It's forever. It's a fact." [20]

Michael was an inspiration to the people working with him by with his strong personal convictions.

"I believe we're powerful, yet we aren't using our minds at full capacity. Your mind is strong enough to enable you to attain whatever you desire." 5

Stay humble

Many who came across Michael Jackson was how shy gracious, courteous, and humble his personality was. They couldn't comprehend why an individual who had accomplished many things and had such talent had no self-confidence to compete with him. However, Michael realized that being "the most outstanding" meant setting the bar high and reaching without thinking you were superior to anyone else. His skills and ambitions were both his teachers and his talents that he used to serve them and when they recognized his efforts with the adulation of millions, he was deeply honored and honoured. He never felt superior to anyone else.

"People would stop by me and ask, you know, do you think you've got a talent?' or 'you are gifted. I'm reminded my mom who is extremely religious and always tells that we should always be thankful to God for His blessings, and to thank Jehovah God to give you your talents and ability. This isn't our fault and comes God's. Therefore, we were always humbled by people who receive acclaim." 21

Michael would always remind the world that his talents was not his, and that it was the result of a gift. His compositions were not his own They came taken from the heavens. His task was to take them in into a new form. Michael was an extremely humble man, and he didn't even claim the credit of his compositions.

The Leçon of his Secret

The mind is a motor which is a creative engine which can be taught to do amazing things. Making goals and setting them can set the direction of the mind. Faith in them, with not any doubt at all, keeps the mind at the subconscious and conscious levels active, always trying to bring the goal to fruition.

Visualization, meditation dreams books, as well as positive affirmations can help push the mind along its journey. The mind is a horse that through the process of training and mentorship can be used to its fullest potential and take you on an amazing creative, enchanting journey. Start making dreams and set goals that are extraordinary, and remind yourself that you are able to achieve whatever you wish to achieve.

*****

Chapter 4: Abandon To The Creative Powers - Descover, Do Not Create

"I'm only the point from that they are born and it's an amazing thing. It's extremely spiritual. It's like sitting under an oak tree and watching a leaf fall before looking to grab it, it's so amazing." 22

The art of writing music and dancing were both spiritual events for Michael because he truly believed that he was in touch with the Divine. He believed that the compositions he wrote were gifts that were already present that were composed prior to the time he was born, in the process of being discovered. His role consisted of opening his eyes to adjust his earsand take in. Michael even admitted to feeling uncomfortable for having "Written Michael Jackson" written by Michael Jackson" in the middle of his music, because Michael felt he just transcribed the music in his mind. Michael Jackson is thought to be an artist of genius, however Michael's creative genius was not due to thinking, but from being free of thinking. He let the music and dance, express its own ideas.

Always Be Ready

Michael considered himself an unwavering servant to the creativity of God. He was always on call 24 all day long in the event that God wanted to grant him the latest song idea or melody or dance moves. Michael was carrying an audio tape recorder throughout the day. If something occurred to him in his head, he would need to capture it. Since Michael was often able to listen to the song in its entirety which means all the instruments and vocals, he would capture not only the vocals but also the beat, strings, the bass and the guitar, all while utilizing his beatboxing ability (which was demonstrated by him performing "Who Are You?" during his Oprah Winfrey interview.)

The very first samples of his work were recorded that he utilized to create the final product. If he began to get lost within the studio when he was working on tracks, he'd return to the tape recordings and then listen again. He would instruct the musicians in the studio not to think too much or overcook the tune and let the original idea be heard.

When Michael was living at home with his parents Encino the city of Encino, he would often take a break from his work and rush to his room. His mother said that she was aware of what Michael was discovering something when she could hear the cries of joy echoing throughout the home. He loved it the moment that something happened and if it enthralled him, he was sure that it would affect others. To the very final the day, he served as an ally to the creative power. In the stage of creation for The This Is It concert in 2009, Michael was constantly adding fresh, innovative concepts for the production. Since the budget was already high, director Kenny Ortega had to ask Michael to slow down. Michael laughed and replied,

"But Kenny, God channels this into me at night. I'm unable to rest because I'm too charged."

Ortega said, "But Michael, we must finish. Why can't God take a break?" With Michael's renewed excitement at the prospect of receiving such innovative ideas, he responded with a reference to his old rival,

"You don't know the meaning of my words. If I'm not here to get these thoughts, God might give them to the Prince." 23

Create an Creative Environment

A good song can be heard anytime and Michael was aware of this. To increase the chances of success He believed that creating a welcoming environment would make the music to play more louder. For Michael the self-made realm of imagination and wonder, referred to as Neverland was his most popular destination. Michael bought the ranch of 2,700 acres in 1988, and began making it a place where the child inside could be free to roam. Michael believed that, with the child's mind the creative process was as simple as tapping the tap. To be happy and to be awed by joy is a sign that you are on the right track to creating the most amazing things. He added that children are geniuses in their creativity but, unfortunately many people lose their ability to create when they reach the age of. He was aware that if he held the mindset of a child the creative abilities of his could continue to flourish and allow him to think creatively and solve issues.

"The magic of wonder, the mystery and the innocence the child's heart can be the seed of inspiration which will bring healing to the world. I truly believe in that." 24

Michael decorated his home and the grounds with life-size statues of cartoon characters, kids, Star Wars villains, and movie icons like Bruce Lee and Marilyn Monroe. He would chat with them and ask them questions and even sing to them. They were his springboard , and were never able to doubt his theories.

The zoo was created that included giraffes and tigers and Llamas. He also had steam trains that was able to take him and his guests to a tour around the vast ranch. There was an arcade for video games, a movie cinema, and, perhaps the most amazing of all the theme park. Michael was fascinated to watch children play and explore the world. Even more than that, he was awed by the sparkle in the eyes of an adult when they take a break from being a adult, even if just for a short time and become a child again.

His amazing 'Neverland' was created because of the enormous wealth he amassed, but Michael would always tell people that you don't have to construct the world of Neverland to discover the voice of God.

One of the easiest ways that Michael did to listen to the amazing songs was to climb up a tree and gaze up at the stars. Michael could hear those songs "Black or White" "Heal the World," "Will You Be There," and "Childhood" as he sat high on his wish tree. Michael was at peace up there far from the problems of the world and the music was heard.

Feel, but don't think
"Don't compose the song. Don't create anything. Let the song come up by itself. This is my rule." 22

Michael's original dance and music was something he learned by feeling, not thinking. He viewed creativity as taking a plunge into a pool of water, experiencing its flow, the touch and letting it guide you to where it would like you to take you.

"Because I do my best to not invent, I attempt to find out what's already there, and I'm figuring out where the song's intentions are to take it." 22

The track "Billie Jean" continued to be a source of inspiration for Michael even after it had been composed. When he was tasked with composing the sequence of dance moves for his Motown 25 performance, Michael was so focused on rehearsals with his brothers that he had not made any plans. On the night prior to the performance, instead of calling any of the numerous choreographers he knew instead, he was listening to the music as it dictated the dance. In his kitchen alone and listening to the music in full-blast, Michael discovered the routine.

"I allowed it to talk to me. I heard the beat and I put on the hat of a spy and began to move and pose in a 'Billie Jean beat create the movements. I felt like I had to let it make itself." 5

Michael found it was time to unleash the moonwalk. which was a dance step that he decided not to include in The Beat It or Billie Jean short-films was now all set to be released. The three spins, and the toe freeze was Michael creating an exclamation mark. However, it wasn't an intentional decision, it was merely the way he felt it was necessary.

"Thinking is the most common mistake an artist can make. You must be able to feel." [25]

Michael often shook his head whenever he saw a dancer making a list of numbers to themselves while they danced. Sometimes, he even saw the dancers mouthing the numbers. Dancing for his music was all about letting the beat influence your movements until you became an actual embodiment of the tune.

"You are the bass, you are the fanfare, and you transform into the clarinet and the flute and string." [25]

Do not overcook it to perfection.

Michael had a tendency to be a perfectionist however, he knew when something is good it's best not to alter it. When he recorded the track "Black or White" the first rendition was so perfect, it was the last time he recorded a song. He was awed by the rawness of his vocals, because it was a song was inside his head for many years and finally sung it. It's the same with the bridge rap. Co-writer of the track, Bill Bottrell, wrote and recorded the rap portion to Michael's attention. The song was a hit with Michael, and he claimed that it would be a good addition to the album. The happy Bottrell declared that he'd engage a professional rapper make it better. Michael was not interested. The song was flawless in his head but someone else's interpretation of it could ruin the original interpretation of the song's creator. Bottrell was stunned, he wasn't a rapper. He was a white middle-aged man who wore glasses and beards of the southern style. Being recognized as the rapper in a song which would be Michael's biggest global hit, was the ultimate dream of many. At Bottrell's urging that his name be recorded with the name "L.T.B." on the credits of the song.

Use the dark to feel the Music

In the studio, as Michael was working on his voice track audio engineers and the producers could only see a glimpse of Michael's shining star. Michael's space was dark, with only some light shining above the microphone. When the music was playing, Michael would dance in the darkness, absorbing the music, letting the emotions rise up. Michael would then walk into the white light to release his emotions before returning to the darkness. For people who worked with Michael it was a remarkable transformation to witness. Michael's voice in his speaking was soft and gentle that the intensity he displayed in songs such as "Dirty Diana" could make the hairs on their necks rise. It was all one of the aspects of spirituality that fueled his creative genius. Michael was channeling his creative power , and let it work and not himself.

Get Attention

Like the majority of Michael's creations the filmmaker was equally amazed as the other people when he saw the same characters back. Inclusion of the "crotch" grabber within The Bad short film shocked a lot of people in 1987 as well as Michael.

"Martin Scorsese" directed the short film set in the undergrounds of New York. It was up to the music dictate to my what I should do. I recall the man saying, 'That's an amazing take! I'd like to show you it. We pushed playback, and I said "Aaaaaaah!' and did not realize I was doing this. Then everyone else began doing it as well, and Madonna as well. However, it's not at all sexual." 5

In 1993, with the estimated global TV audience in the region of 500 million viewers, Michael was confronted about his provocative behavior from Oprah Winfrey. The embarrassed Michael explained the move. Michael went over the situation time.

"I believe it occurs in a subliminal way. While dancing and you're just taking in the music and the rhythm and sounds. If you hear a driving bass and cellos, or strings, you are the emotion that this sound means, and when I'm moving and I say "BAM!" and I grasp myself, and grab myself... It's because of the music which makes me want to perform the move, but it's not that I'm desperate to reach down and that I'm an ideal spot. It's not a thought and it happens. Sometimes, I look back at the video and think... then then I think, 'How did I do this?' I'm in a constant state of mind. rhythm."

In the final moments of the interview Oprah humorously asked whether Michael was willing to "lay aside" the crotch grabber. Being a true servant to the creative power, Michael replied,
"Ask for the to play the." 26

The Leson of his Secret
The best ideas, music and dance exist and need to become known, rather than invented. The job of the artist is to remain open and sensitive to artist's voice, listening to what it's trying to say and then letting them be a physical manifestation of the hidden work. Therefore, tune to the beat and dance flow through your mind.
*****

Chapter 5: Workethic Of A Perfectionist

"Work hard. You have to work as if that there's never a day left. Train. Strive. You need to develop and train your talents to the very highest level. Do your best in your job. Learn more about your area of expertise, better than any other person alive. Utilize the tools you have acquired whether it's books, dancing on a dance floor or an area of water to take a dip in. Whatever you choose to do you want to use it for, the choice is yours." 5

When Michael was hitting a perfect note or execute an amazing dance routine He made it appear effortless, easy to the point that one would believe that it was all divinely-given talent. What they didn't realize was the many hours of hard training and practice that preceded his shows. It wasn't easy. Michael's success was due to a hardworking character that was unique to his peers. The profession of entertainer wasn't just an occupation, it was more of a spiritual passion and one that demanded complete dedication. As a monk, who shuts his eyes from the world and dedicates his whole self in the service of God,

Michael gave himself entirely to his art and his amazing achievements were the reward for his years of commitment.

Be Hard at Work Now, and Reward Will Come Later

Michael Jackson is widely known for his sacrifice of childhood to follow his artistic ambitions. The loss of those precious childhood memories, those which others consider to be a given created a gap in his heart that was a large portion of his adult life striving to make up. In the end, he claimed that he would not have changed one thing. The father he had was an absolute reliable worker and in Michael's expressions, "a genius." His father was the one who inspired him to for hard work.

"I'm quite a lot similar to my dad in a variety of ways. He's very tough. He's a fighter. He's taught us to be strong and sure and believe in our goals. Whatever happens you do, no goal is too for you to reach, and you should don't give up." 20

When Michael was a young boy and he awoke early in the morning to practice his music prior to going to school. His father was sure every boy was up and committed to hone their talents. After school, at the time that the majority of kids would go on bicycles or participate part in a rerun of Lone Ranger, Michael and his brothers would be practicing further. They would usually practice until late at night, and if they didn't perform to their best they might be lucky enough to fall asleep in sleep by 2 A.M. While it was hard but they could clearly see the remarkable progress was being made.

Once one goal was accomplished and the next one was accomplished, the next goal was within sight and the effort never stopped. However, the Jackson Five weren't a quick success, since they took a long time to become "discovered." Their journey began when they began by with local talent contests for amateurs. They soon traded their trophies for cash they earned however it wasn't glamorous as Michael as well as his siblings were seen in nightclubs and stripper joints. It wasn't a suitable place for children to be, however Michael's parents Joseph convinced his family and his wife that every step, however difficult is a step towards your ideal. The ultimate goal was the direction they were headed.

In the midst of five years' hard work traveling across the country in a van from location to location, fame was in the beck and call. Michael's work ethic had changed him from a child who could write notes to a star. His talent on the video of his audition presented by Berry Gordy left no room for further refinement. Michael had already been a professional at age nine. He was an "old soul with a youthful physique." Jackson Five Jackson Five were signed on the moment then Berry Gordy threw his entire label behind Michael and his brothers. It resulted in three top-groove records in the same row. In fact, it was their dedication to the cause that brought the band from a solitary performer in the woods to global praise.

Get the world to pay attention
Michael has always held a particular idea in his head: Michael always wanted to be the best entertainer ever. He was better that

James Brown! More famous than Beatles! Much more famous than Elvis Presley! After the excitement from The Jackson Five waned, he thought that the world was ignoring his name, and that his enthralling vision was in peril. According to The Los Angeles Times' Reporter Robert Hilburn stated of this period, "Through much of the 1970s the group seemed to disappear. It appeared that they were done. It was a an enormous impact on Michael and the fact that Michael was loved by the entire world, but was in a sense , rejected." 27

At the age of fifteen Michael's most recent Jackson Five album G.I.T. Get It Together was released in the hopes that fans would love the album, possibly pushing him back up to number one once more. The album totally failed not charting within the UK and barely making it onto the Billboard Charts at number one hundred. Michael felt devastated. He was among the artists who had ended up, not able to make a profit like they used to and relegated to performing matinee shows for visitors in Las Vegas. He claimed that he believed that he and his brothers were turning into an "oldies" group that played songs from the past to a public who were no longer interested in hearing the latest songs. However, the album had one track that Michael was certain was something he could use. "Dancing Machine" an upbeat song with a mid-tempo beat and stunning horns, had the potential for chart success in the event that the public would be attentive.

Michael was astonished by the amazing street dance "The Robot" and was able to begin to perfect the dance. The only difference was that he did not work under the instruction of his father, or as an manager for Motown Records; it was Michael Jackson alone, taking charge of a career that was stagnant. Michael Jackson spent his spare time working on his dancing, perfecting it and creating it as his own.

The brothers performed on the live program Soul Train, and when the song reached the instrumental break point, Michael let loose. He appeared to be as if he was possessed, swinging the body around before magically floating around the stage. The audience was riveted. The Jackson Five performed the same show on various television shows, and then, suddenly, everyone talked about them. It's a return!

The track became a massive success, and Michael's impressive moves helped to spark an explosion of break dancing that was to follow. Profiting from the popularity, Motown Records decided to name the Jackson Five's upcoming album Dancing Machine, meaning that the song is featured in 2 Jackson Five albums.

Feeling energized by the rising success that Michael was proud of He wanted to have more control of his career. Songwriting gave Michael as well as his siblings to create their own style and to compete with the newer artists who were creating their own music. Michael spent hours creating music demos of his own in his home studio. He then presented them to his bosses hoping they would love the songs and allow them to be featured on their forthcoming album. The new tracks were suspicious of they inquired of Michael who wrote the songs. Regardless of Michael's assertion that the tracks were actually his and that they were his own, they informed Michael that their own team composed of professional songwriters was far more than enough. Michael had only one option and that was to leave Motown Records forever.

Break Free and show Your Talent

Michael along with his brother, with the exception of Jermaine left Motown Records and joined Epic Records in 1975. (Jermaine got married to the daughter Berry Gordy, the President of Motown Records, and stayed because of this.) The decision to leave Motown was a chance to develop their artistic skills and to re-imagine their style. Despite achieving a massive hit through "Dancing Machine" they Jackson brothers were, at present, referred to simply as The Jacksons needed to convince the masses with one song at a. Their previous two albums were mixed reviews as well as Epic Records was even wondering whether they should keep the Jacksons to record a third album. While their backs were to the wall again, Michael and his brother Randy took a rabbit from the hat, and composed the massive hit song "Shake Your Body (Down to the Ground)," which was featured on their album Destiny. At the age of twenty, Michael's voice was no longer displaying the adolescence suffocation, and his unique voice made people reconsider the person they wrote off.

Is this Michael Jackson? Wow He sounds so great.

The multi-talented superstar was beginning to show up, and relying on his gut instincts, he realized it was the right time to go on his own.

Make Headway in the Industry

In 1978, Michael discovered Quincy Jones, the person who would transform his talents from a talented child actor to an internationally acclaimed recording artist on the set the film The Wiz, a big-screen version of the Broadway musical. Quincy Jones is the director of the musical in this beautiful adaptation of L. Frank Baum's The Wonderful Wizard of Oz and the Michael was a young Michael was the fun-loving role of "Scarecrow," staring alongside his idol Diana Ross as "Dorothy." Alongside Michael's incredible dancing and singing, Quincy saw something else that was special about him: his remarkable determination to succeed.

"He was always well-prepared. He was on time at five A.M. for his scarecrow makeup appointment and had every step of what he was required to know memorized and prepared for any shoot. He was also familiar with every dance step as well as every line of dialogue and all the songs' lyrics that was performed by the entire Production." 12

Quincy was approached by Michael to let him know of any producers who could be interested in making their next project. In observing Michael's talent and dedication to his work, he grabbed the chance. "What do you think of my abilities?" he asked. Quincy was aware the fact that Michael had a character who had an amazing driveand was determined to prove himself.

Be interested in learning
While working with the famous Quincy Jones, and masterful sound engineer Bruce Swedien, Michael was the person with a million questions. The musician wanted to learn how

operated with the faders, the reason why a particular microphone was chosen and how they achieved this effect using that guitar. His desire to know was a constant source of inspiration. Michael's determination for excellence was not restricted to just dancing or singing; He was determined to excel in every field. Michael was never the type to be a diva, nor did he complain about his work schedule, since Michael always enjoyed being challenged and was open to the demands of his peers.

The Rod Temperton composition "Lady In My Life" Michael's voice was good however he did not have the intensity Quincy desired. He pulled Michael offstage and told him, "I want you to beg." He guided Michael into the meaning behind the lyrics and explained that in the final section it's supposed to be about the man who begs his lady to remain. The shy and painfully shy Michael was willing to spill his heart out and he was not going to let anyone to be able to see him.

Instead of turning out the light, Michael asked that the curtain be drawn over the control room to ensure that no one Quincy or Swedien could be able to see Michael. The studio was dark and silent, Michael channeled the desperate crying.

"Lay again with me! Let me touch you , girl! Let me relax!
All over! All over! All over! All over! All over! All over! All over. Whoo!
You're my girl! You're my laaaaaaaady baby. Hee!" 28

The performance of Michael was so stunning, Quincy said, "That's an end."

Be humble, while taking the Lead

After three incredible albums which included Thriller, Michael felt that it was time to move on from Quincy to follow his own path. Quincy may have felt like he was being ignored however that wasn't Michael's intent. Brad Buxer, Michael's talented music producer and keyboardist explained the reasons they broke up in an interview he did for Black or White, the Michael Jackson fan magazine Black or White. "Let me clarify:

Michael was not mad at Quincy. He always had admiration for Quincy as well as an enormous amount of respect for him. However, with Dangerous, Michael wanted to manage the process of creation From A-Z. In essence Michael wanted to be the boss of his own. Michael was always a very independent person He was also determined to prove that his success did not happen solely due to one individual that was namely Quincy." 30

Michael formed a group of producers and musicians to provide him with a fresher and, more importantly, a new sound. Following the huge success and recognition Michael had earned as a musician, he needed to instruct people around him to "tell the truth" and help him when necessary. Teddy Riley, the creator of the "New Jack Sound" Teddy Riley, recalled the directions Michael gave him during his interview with HipHopWired.com in 2009.

"Listen I'm going to need to make me into an artist who is new. I'd like you to get in touch with me, I want you to critique me I'd like you to make a comment, and I'm asking you to

provide me with the fullest amount of praise."
30

In a short time, everyone discovered that Michael did not have an ego. The studio was a community where it was impossible to find a voice that was too tiny for Michael to take in. Michael was a hard worker creating scores of tracks for his Dangerous album, often even sleeping in the studio. The studio was filled with tension and Michael was able to release steam.

Bring Fun to the Mix

Contrary to Joseph Jackson, who rehearsed his kids using a strap in his palm, Michael believed that a enjoyable environment would yield better outcomes. The studio office was stuffed with toys. The Nintendo as well as Sega were placed in the studio ready to fight each other big child at the recording studio. When the recording process to record the History album began around 1994 Michael became astonished to find out that a few of his crew had never had seen Jurassic Park, and organized to have a private film screening in Sony Studios for himself and his crew. How was he able to work with someone who didn't have a clue about Jurassic Park? After his sibling Janet presented her live show into town Michael offered everyone seats and told that they should take the night off and work on his own. The next night, they saw an unidentified man wearing robes with a long beard, and who was dancing in the background. This couldn't be possible? But who else would dance as fast? The smiling Michael smiled at them and kept on dancing and gave them some things to chat about following day when they got back to work.

Audio engineer Rob Hoffman revealed that Michael's fun-loving nature was also employed to deal with a rude producer whose sour manner was not a good fit with the group. "Rather rather than cause a fuss or dismiss the producer, Michael called him to his office and one security personnel put a pie in his face. The incident was not a reason to take further action." 31

Get married to your craft
Michael had a remarkable talent and he recognized that it required his total

dedication to reach his goals in the stratosphere. He noticed how when his brother got married young, and starting families the pursuit of music and growth as an artist was put on the priority.

Jermaine has spoken about this in his biography of his older brother You Are Not Alone. "Michael was committed to his craft, and he was puzzled by the fact to think that women could be allowed to stand in the way of our music. Michael would always state"My wife is my instrument and I'm married to my work.'" 18 The consequence of this decision was a lot of loneliness. For Michael this is a difficult pill that was worth taking to be one of the greatest of his generation.

11 years later, after Thriller, Michael did marry after falling in the love of Lisa-Marie, the daughter of Elvis Presley. The two shared a wonderful bond together, and Michael seemed to be the most happy person ever. Although Michael loved his wife and his relationship with her work was never over. When he started making his History album back in 1994, she soon discovered that

Michael was blinded all hours of the day, committing every minute to the creation process. She felt snubbed and was required to read the news to discover what Michael was doing. Lisa-Marie was divorced in 1996 and cited "irreconcilable disagreements."

Despite the turmoil of Michael's personal family life History is an amazing hit, with two US top-ten hits and Michael's greatest UK success that he has ever had "Earth song." Michael began his world tour in 1996, which drew more than 4 million people which made it the largest ever tour by one artist on his own. Lisa-Marie and Michael were friends even at a distance, having feelings for each other as well as Michael kept a photograph of her by his bed until his passing.

The Leçon of his Secret

Put your blinders on and get going. If you do not do all to the best of your ability, you'll not know how proficient you are, or just how far you'll get. Similar to an engagement, your business requires your total dedication and a commitment to quality time for success. Michael was aware of this and gave his objectives the respect they merited and, just like a relationship worthy of fighting for, he did not give up when his career was stalled into the middle of the 70s. Michael was able to make it work through a fresh way to succeed. Get to work and discover the extent to which you can go.

*****

Chapter 6: Rise Across The Hate

"In the midst of hatred, we have to believe in hope." 32

The greatest achievements are not by hard work however, it is also due to the ability to rise back up regardless of how many times you've been knocked down. Michael's tale is not only one of huge success, but also amazing determination. He was in front of thousands of fans in sold-out stadiums to being before eleven jurors, strangers to decide if he should be imprisoned along with murderers and rapists for the duration of his existence. What could have gone so badly? How did he manage to continue to fight back even when the blows were to be too much for one man to take? The key to Michael's success was his ability to fight on, using a force that his adversaries couldn't comprehend and the power to overcome the hatred.

We are sure it will come.

Michael discovered from his humble childhood from his childhood in Gary, Indiana, that whenever you make a change expect to receive some backlash. When his brothers were playing in their tiny home the other kids would come into the house with rocks and throw rocks at their house. These children considered themselves "equalizers," people who will try to keep you on their level, and even punish anyone who wants to be a success in your life. They would shout at them to stop and would tell them that they wouldn't make it and they should simply give up. Michael discovered that people do not want you to abandon them. They don't want you achieve greatness, but they don't want you to be any kind of success. He was faced with the first resistance that artists often face from the people you are familiar with.

For Michael the dream of success wasn't only his; it was a joint venture between the family. When Michael and his brothers returned from sporting competitions with trophy awards and other kids from the neighborhood were watching as they attempted to downplay their achievements and make them look bad. "You had luck" Or "the other things were awful." Michael revisits this real-life experience in the short film Bad which tells the story of an African-American man in the ghetto who attends an elite school on scholarship. He returns to discover his classmates are also his foes. They mock him, asking him if he's still a bad person.

"You would like to know who's the worst? I'll show you who's not." 33

Michael's answer for the entire world. Instead of responding with violenceor hatred Michael responded by demonstrating his skills. He demonstrated to the world over and over again, that he was not their victim.

Every Good Deed is Punished

The Thriller period was, without certainty, Michael was at the top of his game in the list. He was adored by all and it seemed that if the entire world was united to recognize the potential that only one person could be. He received numerous awards, was honoured in the White House by President Reagan His name was added to the Guinness Book of Records. If there's the cloud, then he made it to the cloud of nine thousand. However, as the old saying is, whatever is up must also fall. Michael's situation was such that he did not have a choice and The media wanted to drag him down from these high peaks. After Thriller it seemed like he had done not do anything right.

The album following, Bad, played like an "best ever"" with five US Billboard number one hit songs. In this respect Michael beat the record of Thriller since no one else had achieved this with just one album. This feat could easily be a contender for "Album of the Year" at the 1988 Grammy Awards, but the same academy that gave the artist the eight Grammy Awards for Thriller was now leaving Michael totally empty handed. Michael attended the awards ceremony performing live in front of an academy. However, he was forced to remain in the room as he was unable to win any categories which he was nominated and was completely embarrassed. There were some within the public who enjoyed a fervent attack on Michael. A poll conducted by readers of Rolling Stone magazine in 1989 was a vote to name Michael as the "Worst Male singer" as well as "The Most Unwelcome Return." What was Michael done to merit the aforementioned criticism? Michael returned to the home at Gary, Indiana, being attacked by rocks because he continued to sing the Creator's voice and delight the people.

How to deal with rejection

Michael was a human being, and thus not immune to the criticism that he faced. It was painful for him sometimes deeply however his goals that he humblely served and humbly pursued, demanded him to overcome the negative emotions of humankind. Michael believed that one could determine how you think about things. Your feelings reside within you, and, like an emperor who chooses who is allowed into his home, Michael could choose what feelings he experienced. Meditation was his method to do this, a powerful method to regain his spirit after being confronted by the dark human side.

"When I'm feeling down, I begin to think about the good times that boost my mood. I do this in the night when I'm feeling low on myself. I imagine the most beautiful thoughts in my head about a wonderful experience, and I experience a chemical response that takes over my body, letting me know that I am truly there, and I love this."

Michael took time to let the positive times wash away the bad thoughts that were forming in his mind.

"I am thinking about being in the air, with the wind blowing in my face. I practice it in Africa. I fly up to the highest point which makes me so content in the air and fly." 5

Power of mind that gives Michael wings.

Reconnect with Positive Energy

In addition to contemplation, Michael discovered a sense of peace being surrounded by things that rekindled the belief in magic and also his connection to God. Neverland was a place of imagination, a place where he could be completely detached from the the world and fly like it was during his meditation. The reason he was able to populate his fantasy world with animals and children was because he did not feel that he was being judged by them. Animals couldn't see Michael Jackson as a celebrity or a star He was simply a creation. When they looked at Michael's eyes, they would only see him as a man.

Michael was convinced that they could see him as he really was. Their kindnesses were, therefore, not scrutinized like those of the show business world there was no agenda to hide behind.

Michael enjoyed the same sense of freedom when he was with children. They saw Michael to be Michael Jackson the star, but through their young eyes they were able to look past the image to observe Michael as a normal child, even though he could dance and sing as fast as a frog. Many people ask the reason Michael came up with Neverland but they often view the story through a darker lens and twisting it into something dark. With the difficulties Michael was dealing with following Thriller and with his innate desire to heal and make something, Neverland made perfect sense. It was where Michael felt that he could breathe and stay up.

Dark Days Are Coming

The year 1993 was the time that Michael was confronted with something more serious than a negative review or an enthralling story. The world turned against Michael. A close friend the boy who was thirteen years old, claimed that he had been sexually assaulted by the singer and His father filed an civil action for damages. They sought millions in settlement. Michael's dream of escaping the world became the location that he feared. The police raided his house and turned it upside-down and snatching anything they could and creating an investigation into the crime of removing the king off the seat and put him in an insignificant cell. Michael was adamant about his innocence and, despite his determination to try to clear his name before the courts Michael listened to his legal counsel to settle the civil matter by paying out millions.

There are many who question the reason Michael did what he did and what the legal guidance was very clear. The civil case was too risky. In civil matters the standard of judging does not require a preponderance of doubt rather, based on the basis of the balance of probabilities which is a lesser standard of evidence. If Michael failed in his civil trial, he'd be labeled "guilty" within the eyes of the public and it would be nearly impossible to get an impartial hearing in any legal trial. In addition to the legal complexities to think about, his career was also a matter of concern. Michael was informed that he was not allowed to release any further albums while the legal process progressed and could take 10 years. The possibility depriving him of the ability help his talent or his supporters was too much, and if the money would mean that he could concentrate on his work his music, he would pay the price.

With the family of the boy instantly millionaires due to the settlement of the civil matter the family decided to not aid the district prosecutor, Tom Sneddon, in prosecuting Michael Jackson in a criminal matter. Sneddon could not locate any other children that complained of abuse, so the investigation ended. Much like a villain sheriff in an old Western film, Sneddon swore that he would find Michael someday.

Utilize Music to Release and heal

This album History was Michael's reaction to the allegations. It was also his healingprocess, as the writing of the album helped to restore Michael's confidence. The title of the album was printed on the album's cover as "HIStory" (his account of the events) to inform the world the album was a story of the events. If he had fought his accusers in court his voice would have been quiet, with lawyers representing him. Michael was determined to share with the world the truth and did it by releasing the most candid and autobiographical collection of his life. The album explores a variety of themes. There's the cry for anguish from "Scream," the sigh of sadness from "Stranger In Moscow," the disgust at the plight of betrayal and greed that is in "Money," and the cry of innocence that is "Childhood." Perhaps those lyrics from "They don't care about Us" summarize the pain of his life, and the fight to the end, which is the best.

"I'm exhausted of having to be a subject shame
I'm being thrown into an unpopular class name
I'm amazed that this is the place that I came from." 34

Michael was compelled to feel these songs and let his emotions flow out. After his crew had cleared the studio then he would play the songs in a soaring volume, letting each sound wash over his. It was an escape and cleansing process. He was able to let his feelings out and to feel them move through his body. Music was his drink of choice.

A symbol of his Lazarus-like power to rise from the dead The album was concluded with "Smile," a song of courage in the face of suffering. Written by the idol of his Charlie Chaplin and lyricized by John Turner and Geoffrey Parsons the song laid out the stage for Michael's recovery.

"Light on your face in joy,
Distinguish any trace of sorrow.
Even though a tear might appear to be ever so close
It's when you need to continue to try
Then, smile. What's the purpose of crying.
It's still meaningful
If you simply look at your smile." 35

Michael thought that if he harbored hatred within his heart, he'd be handicapped. The kid who had accused him was controlled by his father and had no hatred toward the boy. He also sincerely forgiven his sister Latoya and, after the accusations surfaced, she stated she was going to "not be a silent accomplice to his actions." Then she admitted that she had spoken under pressure from her husband who was controlling. What is the way that Michael accept such a the act of betrayal?

"I'm ready to forgiving the media, or anyone else. My parents taught me to forgive and love and have that within my soul." 26

Forgiveness, however difficult it may be to swallow was necessary to help him be healed.

Take Charge of Your Issues
In 2003 the D.A. who had tried to arrest Michael back in 1993 got his chance. After 10 years of trying to nab Michael and even traveling to Australia to speak with Michael's teens using his own money He came across the family members who were willing to be witnesses. Michael was detained being charged for sexual harassment of minors. The

family had formed friendship through Michael by way of their son who was a cancer patient. This was something Michael has done all his life, interacting with the most vulnerable and attempting to provide an optimistic light into their difficult worlds. Following the 1993 incident, Michael should have scrutinized the people he invited in his life and, however, since the boy's illness was an extremely serious issue, Michael opened his heart completely trusting. What Michael would discover was the information that the D.A. knew: that the family was grifters.

They were arrested for shoplifting at the department store. But instead of asking forgiveness they were rewarded with a cash reward of $152,000, after claiming sexual assault and battery by security personnel at the store. They also used their son's access to a variety of famous people by using the "we're broke" confession to secure extravagant gifts. However, the most striking aspect of their characterwas when they made it clear to everyone that they did not have insurance for their health, and demanded assistance with their hospital expenses. When the money started coming in they kept the fact the fact that their child was insured by his stepfather's insurance kept a secret.

Other D.A.s who believed that the family did not have credibility they would have dropped the charges. However, not Sneddon. He worked with his family to alter the timeline of events in order to be in line with the fact that they had stated in a taped interview Michael was an angel of God who did not commit any wrong.

With this kind of evidence Michael's legal team been hoping that the case wouldn't be heard in court However, the date for trial was fixed and Michael's future was in danger.

Reunite with Family

For Michael the principles of karma were straightforward: you give energy and affection towards the world, and that's what you will receive in return. He couldn't comprehend how an individual who's entire life was about bringing happiness to others, was facing the prospect of being imprisoned for eighty years because of something he believed that he was incapable of.

"Before I could harm a child, I would cut my wrists. I will never harm children ." 36

Michael made it through the test thanks to the support from his loved ones. His parents, along with his siblings, moved to his Neverland ranch to help keep him going. They would pray and sing in harmony, bridging the gap that Michael's fame accidentally caused. Strangely the trial was the return of family to Michael as, after he left his Jackson household in mid-80s the family reunion was an uncommon event. Michael loved spending time with his family and friends, especially the experience of watching his children grow up acquainted with their aunts, cousins and uncles.

Alongside his immediate family members, his extended family and the crowd were with him throughout the entire process of the way, welcoming Michael with cheers as he left his Neverland gates, and also when they arrived in the courts. As Michael received the "not found guilty" verdict was handed down, Michael did not feel triumphant, since the trial had brought him to the floor, but as always the case, he proved that a star does not have only talent, but also an incredible power.

"I have my goals I'm a dreamer. It's like I've got an armored suit around me, much like an animal skin." 37

The Leçon of his Secret
Looking for something more than others and constantly striving to get it, can result in resistance. Human nature is such that small-mindedness and jealousy can be a hindrance. Keep in mind that all the greatest athletes have been told that they aren't good enough or they don't have the aptitude. It's part of the process.

If success is achieved it is not uncommon to have more haters than there are people who love the artist. In the time of social media the pressures that are placed on an artist are enormous. However, Michael was confronted with the loss of family members, his home being snatched by the police and the threat of a prison sentence He never decided to throw away the idea. It's amazing the fact that he managed accept forgiveness, recover and keep creating music for the world to enjoy. The power he had was his main motivation and no adversaries could stop him from doing what he was passionate about.

*****

Chapter 7: Mystique Metamorphosis

"To to be loved by someone is an amazing thing. This is the primary reason for me to do this. I'm compelled to do itto provide people with an escape from reality as well as a treat for the ear and eye. It's probably the reason that I'm in this place." 19

Michael was determined to not just be the most famous superstar in the world and the biggest spectacle in the world. A live, breathing, and awe-inspiring show. The cover of his album Dangerous is a summary of his lifeas a mixture of art, oddities, beauty and the mystery. The viewer can take a take a look at the cover in a myriad of ways. It attracts you and, even though there's so much to see there, you're only seeing a tiny glimpse. Michael's greatest reason for his success, his ability to always make people beg for more. The point at which Michael the show ended while Michael the man started was an undefined line. The old saying says, "the show must go on," and in Michael's instance the show was a 24-hour-seven-day event.

Create Mystique

When Michael reached adulthood it was a time of little in the way of mystery for his identity. He was timid and reserved, but after many years of TV appearances and interviews the public believed they had a pretty good idea of what he stood for. How was he able to attract the attention of people who believed they had all the information to know? As a servant to his talents, Michael shied away from the Hollywood social scene. Like many of his peers who went to bars and events was not his idea for enjoyment. His shy personality led to a friend to suggest on the possibility that should he continue in this way, he'd end up similar to Greta Garbo in the 1930s, a famous actress known for her eccentricity than her work. Michael was fascinated. Was he able to change his image from one of shyness to one of intrigue and mystery?

Michael has read about Greta Garbo to find out that her erratic remarks and the desire to stay off the radar resulted in her becoming an one of the top talked about people of the time. Look less, desire more. Michael was thinking about how mystique can be a powerful force and how it can boost his career.

Dress Differently

Eyes are believed to be the windows into the soul. When we look into other's eyes, we are able to connect to them and consider them as a human being maybe even as similar to us. Because of this, Michael took the decision to close his eyes, cutting off the connection and causing us to ask who was he, what was it that was going through his mind and how was he coming from.

The latest addition in that of Michael of the Thriller era was the glasses. Anywhere he went even indoors his eyes were blinded. The golden aviators, together in creating a fashion trend that sparked debate and intrigue. He also appeared to stifle his movements when wearing them, opting to not speak much, and rarely even acknowledge the people who were shouting at him, or to turn his head. He created a sense of mystery and the impression that he was different from the rest and not just because of his ability, but also in appearance and manners. "Playing hard to be a success" led to the public wanting more of him, and with the dazzling album Thriller as well as his music videos and moonwalk, his brand new image seemed strangely appropriate. What the Michael Jackson the world was watching was not the Michael Jackson that they had seen grow to be.

In absence of interviews or public speaking, Michael's sequin glove was his primary way of communicating to the outside world. While his lips were closed and his face apathetic, Michael would raise his glove towards the crowd in a gesture of berserk if be he give them the gesture. There's a famous clip of Michael at a concert in London and a person screaming "He was waving at me! He did not even acknowledge me! I'm shocked that he even did that!" All of this was showmanship, directing his actions, and conveying the impression of a detached and delicate genius. If he's not at the same level as them, he's in a different place like he is in two dimensions at the same time.

Privately, Michael didn't care much about dressing up in fancy clothes. He preferred wearing pajamas in the home or just a simple shirt and black slacks. But when he was out, his attire required to be more imposing than life in order to generate a buzz. Michael's style was outfits inspired by military which was believed to be arousing respect and admiration. Sometimes, he wore garish and extravagant clothes that many would not be capable of pulling it off However, none of them were Michael Jackson. When he attended red carpet events Michael's outfits drew the same attention as women. If he'd walked out wearing a black tuxedo as did the other males they would have questioned whether he was in good spirits. The general public has come to expect a show and he didn't did not disappoint them. Michael even turned his trial in 2005 into a fashion show by wearing a different outfit throughout the trial. The day before the trial of his accuser Michael was dressed in pajamas following his admission to a hospital due to back discomfort. There are theories that Michael was attempting to do this deliberately to take all of the attention away from his accuser, and enthralling people with his bizarre methods.

Be careful not to be exposed to too much light.

The traditional theory is that the greater number of interviews and television appearances an artist makes the more albums they'll sell. However, Michael considered overexposure to be the final blow to an artist. When the public believes they've seen everything, they become exhausted and leave. The length of time required to leave the audience wanting more. When he was asked to appear in ads to promote Pepsi Cola back in 1983, the company made in his contract, that they could not use more than three minutes of his face appearing in the commercial. As if it was a supernatural event, you only got just a glimpse. The result was successful, not only for Michael however, but also for Pepsi Cola, which made it the most popular drink in America in 1984. It was a huge achievement for the business, particularly considering Michael would not drink their drink.

The surgical mask was also incorporated to create a sense of mystery and to prevent overexposure. Michael often wore the mask on tours in order to avoid getting an illness, but as a way to increase the excitement of his live performances. On television, fans would catch glimpses of Michael getting to hotels or airports and, when they finally arrived in the arena, they had the chance to see everything. Nothing was hidden. It was a great way to increase the mystery surrounding the man. How did he change from being so shy to being so outrageously stunning within a day, and go from delicate to a powerfully energetic? This is the question for people who follow him to think about and discuss. The word of mouth is the most effective form of publicity.

Create a Myth about Yourself

In addition to the real tales of Michael engaging with mannequins inside his bedroom, Michael soon added fictional personal accounts to his public image. Michael was influenced by the famous promoter of the 1800s and king of the circus, P.T. Barnum who was a man with remarkable talent in the realm of creating public interest. Barnum started with a museum of strange things located in New York, which included hoax-based specimens like a creature that had an animal head, and the tail of an animal. Barnum would inform his critics that the hype was fine even if it wasn't true and if the public still received the most value for their the money. "I don't believe in swindling the public however, I do believe in first appealing to them and then satisfying them."

Barnum began to promote his extraordinary talents before launching the show he described as "the most spectacular show in the world," the Barnum & Bailey Circus. The autobiography of Barnum sold out the roof. Then to ensure that his fame would increase more, he surrendered the copyright so that print shops across the country could sell the book. According to some, it was the most popular book in America in second place in importance to Bible. At the period, Barnum was considered the most famous person around the globe. Michael was fascinated by Barnum's life and his talent for publicity stunts and then began writing stories that would get the world talking.

Make Yourself Sellable as Otherworldly

Michael was a patient of the Hyperbaric Oxygen Chamber in his treatment of third-degree burns to the head in 1984 (the result of a firework that ignited the hair of his subject while filming the footage for a Pepsi commercial.) As he looked over the hi-tech treatment bed, Michael was asked if he would like to purchase one. Michael was enthralled by the idea and it stayed in his mind. A few months later, Michael made the decision to write a story about the story. He approached The National Enquirer, and proposed the idea of a story. They were going to inform all the people on earth that Michael sleeps in an oxygen chamber with the intention of extending his life up to 150 years old. Michael was adamant that his name "BIZARRE" must be used on the front page. The National Enquirer agreed, but they deemed Michael's Polaroid images to be substandard. Michael was not keen to be taken off the front page and thereby losing his front page, agreed to have an experienced photographer take further photographs of him inside the machine. The story was published through international news outlets, and they took note of the report. Michael was the cause of a flurry of conversation, and caught his own family members off by surprise. Michael was thrilled by the response and, considering his Bad album only a year away Michael was the most talked about man on the planet. He enthralled the world with his eccentricities by telling tales of wanting to purchase an elephant's bones, of wanting to buy Elephant man's bones. He also talked about bathing in mineral water and living by eating exotic flowers.

Michael's visual side of his Barnum-inspired antics was that of his partner and friend, Bubbles the chimp. Michael even brought Bubbles to press events. The chimp's fame spread throughout the world as was the query frequently asked whenever Michael was in public "Where do you find Bubbles?" No matter the things Michael accomplished artistically it was clear that he had secured his status as the most talked about man around the globe in all aspects, both good and worse.

Maintain Control

In the year 1993 Michael realized that his stories had gone overboard. Michael didn't admit to orchestrating the stunts however, he wanted people to perceive him as a normal person. Through Michael's Heal the World campaign, Michael was making himself known as a human rights activist. He was spotted in public without sunglasses and the gloves were removed, his lighter skin was believed to be due to Vitiligo (a complexion pigmentation condition) in his candid and empathetic appearance on Oprah Winfrey. Michael's latest PR campaign was successful and the album Dangerous nearly an entire years after it was released, returned to the top ten of charts in America.

Change the way you look

Michael Jackson wanted to be loved and appreciated by all people. He believed that he was an international citizen, and a part of a single race; humanity. The plastic surgery was initially conceived as a way to improve his appearance, and to alter his nose to make it more proportional to his appearance. At the beginning, Michael's work was on the right spot. When he was in 1983, ladies loved his work and men wanted to emulate his style. Michael was able to create a stunning look that was sexual but not threatening. Some believe that Michael's blend of masculine and feminine beauty was what allowed white people who were once hesitant to accept the image of an African American as their idol. However, Michael was never the definition of a "black artist" and viewed himself as so distinctive that identifying him with an era or group was off-putting. Michael's appearance began to reflect his beliefs. Michael wasn't looking to appear white, but instead seeking to be race-neutral.

When Michael released his movie Bad In 1987, the look of his face transformed dramatically and his face was leaning more towards an Latino appearance instead of African American. Michael's brown skin tone was now the creamy, tanned look. His hair was curly, but was noticeably longer. The world was witnessing something that it had never witnessed before, the transformation of the human face. For Michael his face, it was a thing that could be created, changed, and redefined; the perfect canvas to his work.

It will become indefinable

In the 90s Michael's skin tone changed to porcelain white, with his makeup was feminine and chic. Many of his fans were curious about the reason Michael changed so drastically.

"I believe that it is the source of... the nature." 38

Like Michael's music Michael considered his look to be a reflection of the voice of God. The way he sported his look might have shocked America however in Asia his look was consistent with what was considered beautiful by many. The single's cover "You You Aren't Alone" showcases a very Japanese like Michael who is neither totally male or female. His black, thick hair is straight and straight, the eyebrows are extremely small, the lips are a reddish hue and his eyelashes long and curly. However his jaw is masculine and square, and his sideburns indicate in length to his ear. This picture is probably the best illustration of his transformation. He had accomplished his dream of becoming raceless, a appearance that all the world could see a piece of themselves.

Do you think it's a success or a failure?

The effect that Michael's fanciful stories and constantly changing appearance resulted in his record sales is a matter of debate. The United States, it appeared that Michael's changes irritated the general public. But in the rest the world, his acclaim was only growing. The 1995 History concert tour around the world was one of the largest ever as a solo performer and it was achieved without a tour of North and South America. After Michael's death in the year 2009 It was apparent that America accepted the death of Michael and his albums being in nine of the top ten slots in the iTunes album chart. Beyond Michael's lifetime and even in the current century, there's no doubt that he'll be the subject of debate. In this manner Michael's mystery and metamorphosis that transcends race age, gender, and age has earned him popularity for decades to in the future.

The Leçon of his Secret

"The "it element," the thing that connects people's eyes to a celebrity and keeps people talking about it, is made into a personality through clothes, mannerisms and stories of the fantastical. Metamorphosis and mystique can create a show by themselves. Being indefinable allows an extensive range of people to discover something they can identify with and be a part of.

*****

Chapter 8: Career

Michael Joseph Jackson[9][10] was born into the world at Gary, Indiana, close to Chicago on the 29th of August the year 1958. The 11-year-old was the eighth of ten children from Jackson's family. Jackson family, a typical African-American family that lived in a house with two rooms situated on Jackson Street. His mother, Katherine Esther Jackson (nee Scruse) played clarinet and piano, attempted to become a nation or western performer, and was employed in part-time positions at Sears. 15 years ago, she was a Jehovah's witness. His father, Joseph Walter "Joe" Jackson was a former fighter and crane manager, worked in the U.S. Steel and played guitar in a local musicality and blues group, called the Falcons which helped increase the family's earning capacity. Joe's great-grandfather, July "Jack" Gale was an US Army Scout, and there was a family legend that said the man was also an Native American medication man. 19 Michael was raised with three sisters (Rebbie and La Toya as well as Janet) as well as five brothers (Jackie, Tito, Jermaine, Marlon, and Randy). Sixth sibling Marlon's twin Brandon died within a short time after his birth. [20]

When they were in 1964, Michael as well as Marlon were part of the band Jackson Brothers, a group formed by their dad that included Jackie, Tito, and Jermaine as reinforcements performing congas and tambourine. [21][2222 Michael stated that his dad had informed him that his nose was "fat nose",[23and then actually and honestly did not treat him with respect during rehearsals. Michael recalled the fact that Joe often used a seat with the belt in his hands while he and his friends were practicing, and prepared to block any mistake. [16][2424 Joe was aware that he regularly whipping Michael. [2525 Katherine claimed that, even though the practice was later seen as a violation but it was an acceptable method of training children when Michael was growing up.

[26][2727 Jackie, Tito, Jermaine and Marlon denied that their father was a dictator and stated that the whippings and slaps, which were more serious focused on Michael as he was more young, helped keep them in check and safe from trouble. [2828 Jackson claimed that his childhood was lonely and lonely. [29]

In 1964 Michael began to impart lead vocals Jermaine The group's name modified to be the Jackson 5. The group was in the midst of a contest when, on January 15, 1965 group was awarded an ability contest; Michael moved to Robert Parker's 1965 song "Barefootin'" and sang the Temptations' "My Girl". In 1966 through 1968 The Jacksons 5 visited the Midwest They often played at dark clubs , referred to as the Chitlin Circuit, which was the early representatives of craftsmen like Sam and Dave as well as The O'Jays, Gladys Knight, and Etta James. The Jackson 5 were also seen in clubs and lounges with mixed drinks in which striptease shows were featured, as well as in local halls as well as primary school dancing. In the month of August, 1967, while on in the East Coast, they won an amateur hour show that ran week-to-week in Harlem's Apollo Theater located in Harlem. [34]

The Jackson 5 recorded a few songs for an Gary record label, Steeltown Records; their first single, "Large Boy", was released in the year 1968. [3636 Bobby Taylor of Bobby Taylor and the Vancouvers took their group the Jackson 5 to Motown after they performed with Taylor in the Chicago's Regal Theater in 1968. Taylor produced a portion of their original Motown accounts, which included the adaptation of "Who's Lovin You". After signing the band's collaboration with Motown and the Jackson family, the Jackson family relocated into Los Angeles. The year 1969 was the time that Motown executives decided Diana Ross should get with the Jackson 5 with the public-mostly to further establish her career in the world of television, thereby removing the final result from their "creation of a line". They Jackson 5 showed up in 1969 at The Miss Black America event, singing a song called "It's your thing". 40. Rolling Stone later portrayed the young Michael as "a amazing artist" with "overpowering vocal talents" who "immediately became the main attraction and lead singer". [41]

In the month of January, 1970 "I Need You Back" became the first Jackson 5 tune to arrive at the top spot on the US Billboard Hot 100; it stayed there for quite an extended period of time. Three more singles by Motown beat the chart: "ABC", "The Love You Save""The Love You Save", and "I'll be There". In May 1971 the Jackson family moved into a massive house that was built on a section of land situated in Encino, California. At this time, Michael was created from young entertainer to teenager idol. From 1972 to 1975 Michael released four studio albums in association together with Motown: Got to Be There (1972), Ben (1972), Music and Me (1973) and Forever, Michael (1975). [4545 "Became There" and "Ben" are the titles tracks of the first two collections were well-received as singles and a front on Bobby Day's "Rockin Robin". [46]

Michael kept in touch with Michael kept up with connections with Jackson 5. [45 They Jackson 5 were subsequently depicted as "a high-tech depiction of dark hybrid artists". They were dissatisfied by the fact that Motown refused to allow the creative input of the group. Jackson's show of their top five songs "Moving Machine" on Soul Train advocated the robot dance. [49]

In 1975 The year 1975, The Jackson 5 remaining Motown. They signed with Epic Records, an auxiliary of CBS Records. They changed their name to the Jacksons. Their younger brother Randy joined the group close to this point; Jermaine remained with Motown and was looking for an independent career. The Jacksons continued to tour the world and recorded six more collections between the years 1976 and 1984. Michael The Jacksons' primary lyrics writer during this period wrote songs such as "Shake Your Body (Down to the Ground)" (1978), "This Place Hotel" (1980) and "Can You Feel It" (1980). [52]

As of 1977, Jackson relocated in 1977 to New York City to play in the role of Scarecrow In The Wiz, a melodic produced composed by Sidney Lumet. The film starred Diana Ross, Nipsey Russell and Ted Ross. The film was an industry fail. The music was arranged by Quincy Jones,who later produced three albums by Jackson solo. In his time during his time in New York, Jackson regularly went to at the Studio 54 club in which he experienced the early hip jumps. This influenced the beatboxing of his songs, like "Working day and night". in 1978, Jackson suffered a nose injury in the course of a dance. Rhinoplasty caused breathing issues that later had a negative impact on his career. The operation was mentioned through Steven Hoefflin, who played the part of Jackson's surgery. [58]

Jackson's fifth collection of his own, Off the Wall (1979) set out his career as an entertainer who was independent and helped him transition from the bubblegum-pop of his youth to more awe-inspiring music. The collection produced four top 10 tracks within the US: "Crazy", "She's Out of My Life" and the chart-topping singles "Don't stop until You Are Enough" along with "Rock together with You". The album debuted at third place in the US Billboard 200 and sold around 20 million copies around the world. In the year 1980, Jackson won three American Music Awards for his performances work including Favorite Soul/R&B Album Favorite Male Soul/R&B Singer, and Favorite Soul/R&B single for "Don't stop until You've Got Enough". [61][62] He also was awarded the Grammy Award for Best Male R&B Vocal Performance in 1979 with "Don't Stop until You Reach Enough". The year was 1981 and Jackson won named the American Music Awards winner for Best Soul/R&B Album and the most popular male artist in the genre of Soul and R&B. 64 Jackson believed that Off the Wall ought to have had a bigger impact and is still in the air about achieving expectations for his next album. The year 1980 was the time he received the highest eminence rate in the business of music: 37% discount collection profits. [66]

Jackson made recordings with Queen musician Freddie Mercury from 1981 to 1983, where they recorded recordings of "The State of Shock", "Triumph" and "There must be something else to be a part of This". The songs were supposed to be the collection of two-part harmony simultaneously. However, as stated by Queen's manager Jim Beach, the relationship ended after Jackson brought a llama to the studio to record, and Jackson was angry with Mercury's use of drugs. The tunes were recorded in 2014. [70In the year 1970, Jackson recorded "Province of Shock" along with Mick Jagger for the Jacksons album Victory (1984). in 1982, Jackson recorded "Somebody In the Dark" to the recording of the book of the feature film E.T. the Extra-Terrestrial. Jackson's sixth collection, Thriller, was delivered in the latter part of 1982. It was the biggest-selling collection of the year,[72][73and was later rebranded as the highest-rated collection of all time in the United States[74] as well as the highest-quality collection of all time around the globe and sold an estimated 70 million copies. The collection surpassed it's Billboard 200 outline for a lengthy period and was included within the main 100 of 200 during over 80 consecutive weeks. It was the main collection to make seven Billboard Hot 100 top-10 singles which included "Billie Jean", "Beat It" as well as "Want to Be Startin' Somethin'". [77]

On March 25 in 1983, Jackson rejoined with his siblings for Motown 25: Yesterday, Today, Forever, an NBC TV remarkable show. The program was broadcast on May 16, 1983 to an anticipated audience of 47 million, and featured the Jacksons along with the other Motown stars. Jackson's own performance to "Billie Jean" earned the singer his very first Emmy Award nomination. With an embellished glove with rhinestonesthe actor performed the moonwalk dance that Jeffrey Daniel had shown him three years earlier. it became his signature dance routine. [81The 81 Jackson had initially rejected the offer to appear on the show, recognizing that the fact that he was performing on many TV shows. However, as per Motown the original creator Berry Gordy, he acted to gain the opportunity to perform one-on-one performances. [82The Rolling Stone journalist Mikal Gilmore called the show "extraordinary". Jackson's exhibit was a source of comparisons to Elvis Presley's appearance on The Ed Sullivan Show and Beatles appearances on the Ed Sullivan Show. [83The 83-year-old Anna Kisselgoff of The New York Times expressed her admiration for the extraordinary chance and strategical aspects of the dance. [84"84" Gordy is described as "hypnotized" with the show. [85]

The 26th Annual Grammy Awards, the Thriller film won eight awards and Jackson was awarded an award for his E.T. the Extra-Terrestrial book. The awarding of eight Grammys in one ceremony is a record held by Jackson together with Santana. [63(63) Jackson as well as Quincy Jones won the honor of Producer of the Year (Non-Classical). The Thrill Ride album was named an Album of the Year award (with Jackson as the collection's maker and Jones as co-maker) and the single was awarded the best pop Vocal performance (Male) award for Jackson. "Beat It" was awarded Record of the Year and the award for Best Rock Vocal Performance (Male). "Billie Jean" received the two Grammy Awards: Best R&B Song and Best R&B Vocal Performance (Male) and Jackson as the musician. Jackson as artist and musician and artist, respectively. [63] Thriller was awarded the Grammy for Best Engineered Recording (Non-Classical) and also honored Bruce Swedien for his work on the album. In the 11th Annual American Music Awards, Jackson received an additional eight awards, and was the youngest artist to be awarded the Award of Merit. In addition, he was awarded the top prizes for Favorite Male, Favorite Soul/R&B artist as well as Favorite Artiste of Pop/Rock. "Beat It" was awarded Favorite Soul/R&B video, Favorite Pop/Rock Video, and Favorite Pop/Rock Single. The album was awarded Favorite Soul/R&B Album as well as Favorite Rock Album. The deals for Thriller grew with the introduction of a long-winded music video by Michael Jackson, Thriller which shows Jackson performing on the dance floor with an army of zombies. [89][90]

The accomplishment transformed Jackson into a major force within the world of mainstream society, and established his position to be the "lord of the pop world".

"90" Jackson was the highest status in the business of music at the time he was in his prime, earning about $2 per collection sold (comparable to $5 by 2020) and was making records-breaking profits. Dolls that were displayed following Jackson were sold at stores on May 14, 1984, costing 12 dollars each. At the same year, The Making of Michael Jackson's Thriller is a story about his music videos, was awarded the Grammy award for Best Music Video (Longform). [63] Time presented Jackson's legacy in the era of his time as the "star of radio, records and rock video. A one-man salvaging group for the music industry. A music producer who has been setting the music for 10 years. A singer with the most elegant foot in town. A singer who is able to transcend all boundaries of taste and fashion and diversity too. "[91[91] The New York Times stated, "in the realm of popular music, there's Michael Jackson and there is everyone else". [92]

On May 14 1984 the on May 14, 1984, President Ronald Reagan gave Jackson an honor for acknowledging his support of alcohol and illicit drug usage charity organizations, and also in recognition of his support for the Ad Council's and National

Highway Traffic Safety Administration's Drunk Driving Prevention crusade. Jackson allowed the organization to make use of "Beat It" to promote information on public assistance. [94]

On November 3, 1983 Jackson as well as his brothers joined the forces of PepsiCo in an exclusive arrangement of $5 million that set records for large-scale underwriting (comparable to $12,991,981 by 2020). The principal Pepsi campaign, which was in operation throughout the US from 1983 until 1984, and ended it's "New Generation" topic, also included visits to advertising events, sponsorships and store-based shows. Jackson was a part of the advertisement and suggested using his song "Billie Jean" which was reexamined with new lyrics, as its Jingle. [95]

On the 27th of January 1984 Michael along with other people from the Jacksons recorded the first ever Pepsi business under the supervision of Phil Dusenberry, a BBDO director of the promotional firm and Alan Pottasch, Pepsi's Worldwide Creative Director in the Shrine Auditorium in Los Angeles. At a show that was recreated in front of an audience of over 2,000 the fireworks accidentally set Jackson's hair on fire, which caused extremely charred areas on his scalp. Jackson underwent therapy to hide the scars, and underwent his third rhinoplasty shortly following. [97The 97 Pepsi privately addressed all remaining concerns as well as Jackson agreed to pay an $1.5 million payment to Brotman Medical Center located in Culver City California which is currently shut down. Michael Jackson Burn Center was named in honor of his memory. [98][99(99) Jackson agreed to a third agreement with Pepsi during the latter part of the 1980s, for $10 million. The following mission was a total of 20 countries and offered financial aid to Jackson's Bad collection as well as his 1987-88 trip to the world. Jackson was a promoter and supporter of and various organizations, including LA Gear, Suzuki, and Sony but none of them were as crucial as his ties with Pepsi. [95]

The Victory Tour of 1984 featured the Jacksons , and showcased Jackson's brand new material that was independent to a large number of Americans. This was the last tour Jackson made together with the Jackson brothers. In the aftermath of a disagreement about the show's pass agreements, Jackson gave his portion of the profits of the show, which ranged from $3 million to 5 million to charity. The last performance during the Victory Tour at the Dodger Stadium in Los Angeles, Jackson declared his separation from his bandmates The Jacksons in the song "Shake your body". His benevolent work continued to be evident with the release of "We are in the world" (1985) which he co-wrote with Lionel Richie. helped raise money for the needy across both the US as well as Africa. The song was sold for the sum of $63 millions (identical to $151,593,750 by 2020),[104It became one of the greatest selling singles ever, selling 20 million copies sold. [105] It received the record four Grammy Awards in 1985, including Song of the Year for Jackson and Richie as the song's creators. The project's creators received two stunning American Music Awards respects: one for the creation of the tune as well as another one to being recognized in the USA to promote African thought. Jackson, Jones, and the advertiser Ken Kragen got unique honors for their roles in the composition of the tune. [103][106][107][108]

Jackson collaborated along with Paul McCartney in the mid-1980s and found out that McCartney earned $40 million a year being able to freely use perform other artists' songs. In 1983 Jackson was beginning to purchase rights to distribute other music, however Jackson was cautious about the purchases, offering only just a few many that were offered to him. Jackson's first acquisitions of music inventories and copyrights for melody such as Sly Stone, for instance. Sly Stone assortment included "Regular People" (1968) and the song by Len Barry "1-2-3" (1965) as well as Dion DiMucci's "The Wanderer" (1961) and "Evasion Sue" (1961).

The year 1984 was the time Robert Holmes a Court stated that he was selling an ATV Music Publishing index containing the rights to distribute almost 4000 songs, which included significant portions of the Beatles material. The year was 1981. McCartney was offered the index in exchange for PS20 Million ($40 million). [104][110110 Jackson offered $46 million on the 20th of November the 20th of November, 1984. [109If Jackson and McCartney were unable to make an agreement to buy together, McCartney would have rather not be the sole owner of the

Beatles music and didn't pursue an agreement for himself. Jackson's representatives could not agree on a deal and, in May 1985, remained in talks after spending over $1million, and 4 months of an anticipated amount of effort working on the discussions. When they met in the summer of 1985 Jackson as well as Branca discovered that the Koppelman's and Marty Bandier's The Entertainment Company had made an offer to purchase ATV Music for $50 million and at the beginning the month of august, Holmes a Court reached Jackson and discussions were continued. Jackson's revised offer in the amount of $47.5 millions (comparable to $114,296,875 by 2020) was appreciated as he was able to settle the deal faster, having already completed due diligence. [109Jackson consented to visit Holmes a Court in Australia. Jackson agreed to go to Holmes the Court in Australia in which he was to be at his Channel Seven Perth Telethon. The acquisition by Jackson from ATV Music was concluded on August 10 in 1985. [104][109]

Jackson's skin color was medium brown in his early years, but in the late 1980s, his skin began to turn lighter. The shift in color drew wide media attention, including the notion that he might have dyed his face. The dermatologist of Jackson, Arnold Klein, said he observed the condition in 1983. Jackson had vitiligo. It is which is a condition that manifests as patches of skin that lose their color, as well as dislike of sunlight. He likewise recognized discoid lupus erythematosus in Jackson. He concluded Jackson to have lupus at the time of the year, and also vitiligo in 1986. The vitiligo's unforeseen effects for the body could cause mental stress. Jackson used fair-shaded makeup and possibly skin-dying solution creamsto hide the uneven streaks of variation caused due to the disease. The creams may have helped to smooth his skin and with the help of cosmetics, Jackson could appear pale. [120Jackson said that Jackson claimed that he never intentionally dyed his skin and did not have any control over his vitiligo. He added "When people make up tales that make me feel like I should not be the person I am that harms me. "[121He was a friend along with Klein and Klein's partner, Debbie Rowe. Rowe was later Jackson's second wife and mother of his first two children. [122]

In his account of his life in 1988 and in a 1993 gathering, Jackson said he had two rhinoplasty procedures as well as the dislocation of his jaw was one of the medical procedures, however that's what it was like. He also claimed to have shed a few pounds in the mid-1980s as a result of the change in diet required to achieve the body of an artist. Witnesses stated that he was often drowsy and that they believed that he was suffering from anorexia. Weight loss became a frequent issue and were a frequent problem later on during his time. After his death Jackson's mother said Jackson initially sought treatments that would correct his vitiligo because Jackson would rather not appear like the "spotted cow". She also said that he'd had more than two restorative procedures the doctor claimed, and suggested that he became dependent on these procedures. [125]

In 1986, a number of sensationalist publications declared that Jackson lay in a hyperbaric oxygen room to slow the process of maturing. They also believed that he was sitting in a glass container. The claim was untrue and tabloids discovered that Jackson had spread the news himself. [126] They also revealed that Jackson engaged in female chemical attempts in order to maintain his voice strong and his beard growing wispy. He also engaged to Elizabeth Taylor and potentially had an sanctum for her and also had an operation to correct his eyes. His director Frank DiLeo kept all from receiving them, with the exception of Jackson being in an air chamber. DiLeo said "I did not know if Jackson rests there. I'm not a fan of it. In any event, Michael believes it's likely beneficial to him. He's a health lover. "[127]

When Jackson brought his pet Chimpanzee Bubbles to Japan The media depicted Jackson as an optimistic Disney animated character who makes an animal lover. The story was further discovered that Jackson was planning to purchase the bones belonging to Joseph Merrick (the "Elephant Man"). In June 1987 the Chicago Tribune detailed Jackson's marketing specialist who was offering $1 million to donate the bone skeleton for the London Hospital Medical College for his benefit. The college remained on top of the skeleton, but it was not available to purchase. DiLeo claimed that Jackson was an "retaining fascination" with Merrick, "absolutely founded on his awareness of the ethical, clinical, and historical significance."[130]

Newspaper stories inspired the nickname "Psycho Jacko" that Jackson began to hate. According to music journalist Joseph Vogel, the disparaging name first surfaced on The British publication The Sun in 1985. The name's origins stem from Jacko Macaco, the name of a famous monkey who was used during monkey-goading games in the Westminster Pit in the mid-1820s. "Jacko" was used to refer to a monkey in Cockney shoptalk to refer to the general population of monkeys and thus, a skewed significance that explains the name. [132]

The year 1987 was the first time Rolling Stone depicted Jackson as "the unpredictably virtuoso young star, an absolute VIP for the entirety of his entire career living in a world of individuals, characters that are life-sized models, and kids' shows that give endless grain to the sensationalist media... Yet, a youngster in Michael inspires the imagination that is the basis of all the secondary enterprises, and transforms his basic feelings of anxiety and fears into dazzling, hyperkinetic and exuberant music."[128]

Jackson collaborated together with George Lucas and Francis Ford Coppola in the production of the 17-minute $30 million 3D films Captain EO, which ran through 1986 at Disneyland and Epcot as well as later at Tokyo Disneyland and Euro Disneyland. After being removed from the park in the final period of the 1990s it returned at the park's amusement park over a long time following Jackson's death. The year 1987 was the time that Jackson removed himself from his Jehovah's witness group. [135The reason for this was that Katherine Jackson said this could be due to a handful of Witnesses were unambiguously against this Thriller video. [136The film was criticized by Michael Michael had criticized the film in an Witness release in 1984. [137]

Jackson's debut album in a long time, Bad (1987), was a hugely anticipated release as the industry hoped for another huge success. The album was later turned into the main collection , which produced five US number one songs "I Just Can't Stop Loving You", "Terrible", "The Way You Make Me Feel", "Man in the Mirror" and "Grimy Diana". Another track, "Smooth Criminal", was ranked at the number seven spot. [59] Bad was awarded in 1988 the Grammy in the category of Best Engineered Recording - Non-Classical as well as the 1990 Grammy Award for Best Music Video, Short Form for "Leave Me Alone". [63][86(86) Jackson was awarded the Award for Achievement in the American Music Awards in 1989 following the fact that Bad released five top-five singles and became the first compilation that beat all other collections in a very long time and was the most sought-after collection between 1987 and 1988. By the year 2012, the album was selling between 30 to 45 million copies across the globe. [141][142]

The Bad World Tour began on September 12, 1987 until January 14 1989. [143 In Japan the tour saw 14 sellouts and attracted 570,000 people, significantly surpassing the record for an all-in-one tour. The 504,000 fans who attended seven sold out concerts in Wembley Stadium set another Guinness World Record. [145]

It was in 1988 that Jackson released his auto-portrait, Moonwalk, with input from Stephen Davis and Jacqueline Kennedy Onassis. The album sold 200,000 copies and was the top position in the New York Times smash hits list. [148Jackson was interviewed by the New York

Times. Jackson discussed his life as a child as well as The Jackson 5, and the brutal treatment he received by his father. Jackson attributed the change in his face to three cosmetic medical procedures: pubescence, weight loss, a rigorous vegan diet, a change of hairstyles, as well as stage lighting. The month of October was when Jackson released a documentary, Moonwalker, which included live-action film and short films with Jackson as well as Joe Pesci. It was distributed in the US it was filmed direct-to-video, and later turned into the cult videocassette. [151][152 The RIAA ensured it was eight-time Platinum. [153]

In the month of March 1988 Jackson purchased 2,700 acres (11 square kilometers) of land near Santa Ynez, California, to build a second residence, Neverland Ranch, for $17 million (identical to $37,200 in 2020). The man created a Ferris wheel as well as a merry-go-round, cinema as well as the zoo. A security crew of 40 stayed on the areas. Then, shortly after was he featured in the most famous Western TV advertisement for the Soviet Union. [157]

Jackson was referred to by the name of"the "Ruler of Pop" and this was a name that

Jackson's marketing professionals took to heart. [24][158][159] In the year Elizabeth Taylor gave him the Soul Train Heritage Award in 1989, she called Jackson as "the true lord of rock, pop and soul. "[160The president George H. W. Bramble named him the title of White House's "Craftsman of the Decade". From 1985 until in 1990 Jackson contributed $455,000 towards the Unisco College Fund.and all proceeds of his hit single "Man In the Mirror" was donated to charities. The interpretation he gave of "You Didn't Exist" during Sammy Davis Jr.'s. 60th birthday celebrations earned Jackson an additional Emmy nomination. [79The 79-year-old Jackson was the most highly rated craftsman in the 1980s. [164]

In the month of March, Jackson restored his agreement with Sony for $65 million (identical to $123,504,764 by 2020) an unprecedented deal, [165beating Neil Diamond's previous restoration agreement in the same year with Columbia Records. The year was 1991 when he released his eighth album, Dangerous, co-created with Teddy Riley. The album was guaranteed to be platinum multiple times in the US and, by the year 2018, was selling 32 million copies around the world. In the US the first track, "Dark or White" was the album's most notable diagramming track that topped the charts at first on the Billboard Hot 100 for a significant amount of time, and also facilitated similar outline shows all over the world. The following track, "Recall the Time" was ranked third in the Billboard Hot 100 singles chart. [171] By the end in 1992 Dangerous became the biggest album of the year , in addition to "Dark or White" was the most popular song of the year in the Billboard Music Awards. The year 1993 was the first time he sang "Recollect the Time" at the Soul Train Music Awards in sitting in a chair and said that the lower leg was curled in dance practice. [172 in the UK, "Recuperate the World" came in at the number. 2 on the outline in 1992. [173]

Jackson founded his Heal the World Foundation in 1992. The foundation brought children who were oppressed to Jackson's farm, where they could enjoy amusement parks and provided a huge amount of dollars across the globe to aid children affected by neediness, war and infected. In July of 1992, Jackson distributed his subsequent book, Dancing the Dream, featuring a variety of songs. His Dangerous World Tour ran between June 1992 to November 1993. It earned him 100 million dollars (comparable to $179,152,269 by 2020); Jackson performed for 3.5 million people in 70 shows, completely outside of the US. 175 percent of the profits were given to the Heal the World Foundation. [176The 176 Jackson transferred the freedom of transmission during the trip the to HBO in the amount of 20 million dollars, a record-breaking deal which is still in effect. [177]

Following the death of HIV/AIDS representative and co-conspirator Ryan White, Jackson begged to the Clinton organization at Bill Clinton's inaugural function to donate more money to HIV/AIDS worthy cause and research[178][179And he sang "Gone too soon" the tune dedicated to White and "Mend the world" in the event. [180The singer Jackson went to Africa in the mid-1992 time frame and on his first visit in Gabon where he was received by over 100,000 people who carried signs reading "Welcome Michael Home Michael",[181[181]] and was awarded the status of an Officer in the National Order of Merit from the president Omar Bongo. [182] During his visit in Ivory Coast, Jackson was designated "Ruler Sani" by a clan leader. Jackson expressed his gratitude to high-ranking officials both in French and English and engraved archives to confirm his authority, and was seated in a magnificent high position while leading formal dances. [181]

In the month of January 1993, Jackson was on stage in Jackson's Super Bowl XXVII halftime show in Pasadena, California. The NFL sought out a big name to ensure that the evaluations remained at a high level during halftime after a decline in numbers of spectators. [184][185It was the first Super Bowl whose half-time execution attracted more attention from the crowd than the actual game. Jackson was on stage to perform "Jam", "Billie Jean", "Dark or White" and "Mend The World". Perilous climbed 90 places on the graph of collection after the performance. [113]

Jackson permitted one hour and half chat for an hour and a half with Oprah Winfrey, on the 10th of February 1993. He spoke about his experiences as a child and the abuse he suffered because of his father; he admitted that he was unable to share many of the things he experienced when he was a kid and claimed that he would often cry from depression. He denied the newspaper stories that he purchased bone fragments of

Elephant Man and snoozed in an oxygen chamber that was hyperbaric, or even froze his skin and also claimed that he was suffering from Vitiligo. Risky was re-introduced within the collections diagram of the main 10 over one year after the publication. [24][113]

On January 23, 1993, Jackson was awarded the following three American Music Awards for his Favorite Pop/Rock album (Dangerous) and Favorite Soul/R&B Track ("Remember that Time") Then he quick to win the International Artist Award of Excellence. He also was awarded the "Remarkable individual Award" at the 35th Annual Grammy Awards in Los Angeles. He attended the event together with Brooke Shields. [188Dangerous won the honors. Dangerous was awarded the Best Voice Performance (for "Dark and White") and the Best R&B Vocal Performance ("Jam") and the Best R&B song ("Jam") in addition, Swedien and Riley were awarded the prize for the Best Engineered Non-Classical. [86]

In August 1993 Jackson was blamed for child sexual abuse by a 13-year-old teenager, Jordan Chandler, and his father, Evan Chandler. [189Jordan Chandler was accused of sexual assault. Jordan stated that Jordan and Jackson were occupied with the display of masturbation, kissing and oral sexual relations. Although Jordan's mother initially let officers know that she did not entirely believe the fact that Jackson was a victim of his own but her position changed after a few days. [191][192The following day, Evan was interviewed about his motive to pursue the charges. Jackson was able to claim that he was the victim of an jealous dad's attempt to bribe his way into paying. Jackson's older sister, La Toya claimed that he was an alleged pedophile. She later retracted her accusation assertion, claiming she was in a position to do it because of her husband's oppressive behavior. Police resounded Jackson's house in August. They saw two genuine huge workbooks that featured youngsters running, playing and swimming in various situations of casual wear. [195The 195 Jackson was unable to know about the contents of the books and was able to ensure that they were in the possession of someone who needed to give them to him . He did not open them. [196Jordan Chandler Jordan Chandler provided police with an image of Jackson's privates. The strip-search was conducted and the legal authorities were of the opinion that the representation did not match. Then, in January of 1994 Jackson privately addressed all remaining issues , revealing an total amount in the range of $23 million. [200] The police have never made any charges against Jackson. In the absence of evidence, without Jordan's permission that Jordan had signed, the state closed its examination on the 22nd of September in 1994. [202]

Jackson was making more time for his medical procedures for reconstructive scalp which he was able to manage due to the Pepsi business accident in 1984. Then, he began to be able to cope with the pressures of sexual assault allegations. On November 12 on the 12th of November 1993 Jackson was forced to cancel the remaining portion of the Dangerous Tour because of medical problems, stress due to the allegations, and a the habit of taking painkillers. Jackson expressed his gratitude to his dear his companion Elizabeth Taylor for help, guidance, and support. The end of the tour ended his relationship with Pepsi-Cola who supported the tour. [204]

In the latter half of 1993 Jackson was engaged his love to Lisa Marie Presley the daughter who was a friend of Elvis Presley, over the phone. The couple was married at La Vega,

Dominican Republic in May 1994, by a common-appointed official Hugo Francisco Alvarez Perez. The media of the newspaper speculated it was an ad-lib technique to divert Jackson's accusations of sexual abuse and to relaunch Presley's career as a musician. Their wedding was just over an entire year after the event, and they broke up from the public in November 1995. [208Then, Presley was quoted as having "hopeless contrasts" when she sought legal separation in the month following and sought to recover her family's name as a settlement. Following the separation The judge Perez stated, "They endured longer than I anticipated they would. I gave them one year. They lasted for one year and an hour. "[206]

Jackson was scheduled to compose tracks for Sega Genesis computer game Sonic the Hedgehog 3 (1994) but he resigned from the project around when the sexual abuse accusations surfaced. The charges were not acknowledged. Jackson was known as a Sonic fan,[210] and collaborated with Sega on the arcade-based game Moonwalker. The motives for Jackson's decision to take off and whether his synthesizers will remain in the game's game has been subject to debate. Sega

Technical Institute chief Roger Hector and Sonic the Hedgehog co-maker Naoto Ohshima claimed that Jackson's relationship was terminated and his music changed in response to the accusations. But Jackson's musical chief Brad Buxer and two different colleagues, Grigsby III and Cirocco Jones, insisted that Jackson's music continued and Jackson was not credited as a musician due to his discontent over the way in which Genesis mimicked his music. [213]

On June 15, 1995, Jackson released the double collection HIStory: Past, Present and Future Book I. The first album, HIStory Begins, is an all-time greatest hits compilation (reissued in 2001 under the title Greatest Hits: HIStory, Volume I). The next collection, HIStory Continues, contains 13 original tunes as well as two cover variations. The collection was ranked at top of the charts and was confirmed to have 8,000,000 units shipped across the US. [214] It's the best multi-plate collection of all time and has the collection having 20 million duplicates (40 million copies) sold globally. [170][215The album HIStory received an Grammy award as album of the year. (63) The New York Times audited the album as "the performance of a musician who's self-centeredness is now threatening his talents". [216]

The most popular track in HIStory included "Shout/Childhood". "Shout" is a double harmony featuring Jackson's youngest sister Janet and Janet, rebukes the treatment by the media of Jackson in the wake of 1993's kid abuse allegations against the singer. The song ranked at fifth place at the top of the billboard hot 100 chart,[171and was an Grammy nomination in the category of "Best Song Collaboration in Pop with vocals". The following track, "You Are Not Alone" has the Guinness world record for the main melody and makes a major appearance at the top of the Billboard Hot 100 chart. [217] It was awarded the Grammy distinction as "Best pop vocal performance" during 1995. [63]

In 1995, the Anti-Defamation League and that's what diverse gatherings said "Jew me sue me, everyone does me/Kick me/Kike me Don't you look dark and white" The first three lines of "They Don't Pay Attention to Us" were considered anti-Jewish. Jackson performed a version that reexamined the words. [218][219]

In late 1995 Jackson was taken to an emergency room after exploding during rehearsals for a broadcast performance, caused by an alarm related to pressure. Then, in November of 1995 Jackson was able to consolidate the ATV Music index with Sony's division for music distribution and created ATV Music Publishing. He was responsible for the business, and he was able to acquire $95 million in cash (identical to $161,348,548 by 2020) and also the rights to additional songs. [221][222]

"Earth Songs" is the 3rd single to be released from HIStory and topped that of UK Singles Chart for quite an extended period of time during Christmas 1995. The song was later the 87th highest-rated single across the UK. 223In 1996, at the Brit Awards in 1996, the performance to the audience of "Earth song" was not a success due to Pulp singer Jarvis Cocker, who fighting Cocker was deemed to be Jackson's "Christ-like" personality. Jackson claimed that the intrusion on stage was "nauseating and a smug coward". [224][225]

The year 1996 was the year that Jackson was awarded an Grammy to be awarded for Best Music Video, Short Form for "Shout" as well as an American Music Award for Favorite

Pop/Rock Male Artist. [63][226226 Jackson progressed HIStory by launching The HIStory World Tour, from September 7, 1996 through October 15th in 1997. Jackson performed 82 shows across five continents, 35 countries and 58 cities to more than 4.5 million fans, which was his most visited to date. The concert grossed $165 million. In the course of the trip to Sydney, Australia, Jackson got married to Debbie Rowe, a dermatology associate who was half-year pregnant with the first of his children. [227The [227] Michael Joseph Jackson Jr. (regularly called Prince) was born to the world on the 13th of February 1997. His younger sister, Paris-Michael Jackson was born within a year of the birth on April 3rd of 1998. [228228 Jackson and Rowe split in 1999, and Rowe gave up custody of the kids in exchange for an agreement of $8 million (identical up to $13,981,822 by 2020). In 2004, following the subsequent accusations of abuse of a child against Jackson and Rowe, she went back in court to seek custody. The suit was finally settled in the year 2006. [229]

in 1997. Jackson came out with Blood on the Dance Floor: HIStory in the Mix in 1997, which included remixes of songs from HIStory and five brand new tracks. The total sales amount to 6 million copies, making it the highest-rated collection of remixes ever. It was ranked top spot in the UK as did its title song. [230 In the US the collection landed at number 24 , and was certified platinum. [168]

Between October 1997 and the end of September, Jackson was working on his 10th album of his own, Invincible, which cost $30 million to create. [231 On June 29, 1999 Jackson took part with Luciano Pavarotti for the War Child benefit concert held in Modena, Italy. The event raised 1 million dollars for refugees from The Kosovo War, and extra assets for the children of Guatemala. The following time, Jackson organized a string to "Michael Jackson and Friends" benefit shows across Germany as well as Korea. The various craftsmen featured included Slash, The Scorpions, Boyz II Men, Luther Vandross, Mariah Carey, A. R. Rahman, Prabhu Deva Sundaram, Shobana, Andrea Bocelli, and Luciano Pavarotti. The proceeds went directly to Nelson Mandela Children's Fund, the Red Cross, and UNESCO. In the months of August 1999 through 2000, Jackson lived at New York City at 4 East 74th Street. [234] As the new century came to an end,

Jackson won an American Music Award for Artist in the 1980s. in 2000, Guinness World Records remembered him for his contributions to 39 foundations, which is more than any other entertainer. [236]

On September 11, 2001, two 30-year anniversary performances were staged on September 30th at Madison Square Garden to check Jackson's 30th anniversary as a self-employed craftsman. Jackson was a part of the show alongside his siblings with a lot of interest starting in the year 1984. The show also featured Mya, Usher, Whitney Houston and Destiny's Child, Monica, Liza Minnelli and Slash. The show's first episode was destroyed with specialized slips and the audience was booed during a speech that was led by Marlon Brando. More than 30 million viewers saw the broadcast of the show in November. After the attacks on September 11, Jackson coordinated the United We Stand: What More Can I Give Benefit Show held at RFK Stadium in Washington, D.C. on the 21st of October 2001. Jackson sang "What more can I give" to close the show. [239]

The release of Invincible was canceled prior to the beginning of a dispute over Jackson as well as his recording label, Sony Music

Entertainment. Jackson was anticipating that he would get the licences would be granted if the managers of his collection return to him by the mid-2000s. Following that, Jackson would be able to move the material in to any extent he wanted to and continue to enjoy the benefits, however, the clauses in the contract made the return date to be a long time to be the future. Jackson was looking for an earlier departure from his contract. The [240] Invincible was released on the 30th of October 30th 2001. It was Jackson's first complete collection in a long time and the last album of his own material during his entire career. It ranked the top of the list out of 13 countries and was able to sell 8,000,000 duplicates across the globe and was certified two times platinum for the US. [168][241][242]

On the 9th of January the 9th of January 2002, Jackson won his 22nd American Music Award for Artist of the Century. In the following year an unidentified proxy mother gave birth to his third child, Prince Michael Jackson II (nicknamed "Cover"), which was brought about by a fake insemination. The 20th of November, Jackson momentarily held Blanket on the railing of his Berlin residence, which was four stories higher than the level of the ground, prompting an extensive analysis in the media. Jackson apologyd to the media for this incident and described it as "a terrible mistake". On January 22 the advertising executive Marcel Avram documented a break of agreement, expressing frustration with Jackson for not performing two concert dates in 1999 that were scheduled. In March the same month, an Santa Maria jury requested Jackson to pay Avram $5.3 million. On the 18th of December in 2003, the Jackson's lawyers did not respond to any requests regarding the verdict and settled the case for an undetermined amount. [250]

On April 24 2002 Jackson appeared at Apollo Theater. The concert was a pledge drive to The Democratic National Committee and previous president Bill Clinton. The money raised could be used to convince people to cast their ballots. It brought in $2.5 million. [252The show was called Michael Jackson: Live at the Apollo and was Jackson's final crowds. [253]

The issue was raised in July of 2002 when Jackson stated that Sony Music executive Tommy Mottola "a bigot, and extremely, shrewd" and someone who exploits dark specialists to benefit himself in the Al Sharpton's National Action Network in Harlem. The accusation prompted Sharpton to create an alliance that would investigate whether Mottola made money off of dark musicians. [254Then, Jackson asserted that Mottola was a fan of his friend Irv Gotti to be a "fat nipper". In response to the attacks, Sony gave an assertion that they were "outrageous anger, resentful, as well as destructive" and defended Mottola as a person who helped Jackson's career for several years. [254Then, Sony has finally said it will not renew Jackson's contract and also guarantee that a special $25 million project had failed due to the fact that Jackson did not want to visit.

Beginning in May 2002 the narrative film crew led by Martin Bashir and Jackson for a lengthy duration. The film, which was aired in February 2003 under the name Living with Michael Jackson, included Jackson hugging hands and discussing doingzed-out actions with 12 year old boy. He claimed that he had no objections about hosting sleepovers for minors or offering his room and bed to different people that sparked discussion. He insists that the sleepovers are not sexual in nature and claimed that his remarks were misinterpreted. [257][258]

On the 18th of November, 2003 Sony came out with Number Ones the biggest hits album. It was certified five times platinum by the RIAA and multiple many times platinum within the UK with deliveries of approximately 2.7 million copies. [168][259]

On the 18th of December 2003 Santa Barbara specialists accused Jackson of seven counts of kid assault along with two other counts for intoxicating minors with hard liquor. [260The defendant Jackson denied the allegations and claimed not guilty. [261261 The People v. Jackson preliminary hearing began on the 31st of January, 2005 at Santa Maria, California, and continued until the end of May. Jackson felt the event was difficult and affected his overall health. If he had been able to, he could have been sentenced to up to the maximum of 20 years prison. On June 13th of the 13th of June, 2005 Jackson got a clean bill of every count. Following the initial the trial, he was withdrawn[264] and was transferred to Bahrain as a guest of Sheik Abdullah. In December 2009 the Federal Bureau of Investigation (FBI) provided records on Michael Jackson. The records revealed the

Bureau's work in the 2005 preliminary investigation and accusations made against Jackson and other revelations. The FBI did not find any evidence of any criminal intent for Jackson's behalf. [266][267]

In April of 2006, Jackson consented to utilize part from his ATV index stake which was at the time estimated at $1 billion to guarantee his $270 million in loans from Bank of America. Bank of America had offered the loans for the purpose of Fortress Investments, a speculation business that buys delayed advances in the previous year. In accordance with the agreement, Fortress Investments furnished Jackson with a second credit amounting to $300 million that included lower income installments (comparable to $385,127,105 by 2020). Sony Music would have the option of buying half his stake, which is approximately 25% on the total for a predetermined price. Jackson's financial chiefs had urged Jackson to sell a portion of his stake in order to stay clear of bankruptcy. The primary residence located at Neverland Ranch was closed to cut costs and Jackson was at Bahrain under the courtesy of Sheik Abdullah the son of the ruler. There were at least 30 , Jackson's representatives weren't paid according to time and were owed an amount of $306,000 as back compensation. Jackson was ordered to pay $100,000 for penalties. [222]

In the middle of 2006 it was revealed that Jackson had signed agreements with Bahrain-based company, Two Seas Records; Nothing happened to the agreement however, and Two Seas CEO Guy Holmes then claimed that the deal was never signed. The following October, Fox News detailed that Jackson was recording in an recording studio located situated in County Westmeath, Ireland. It wasn't clear the exact nature of the project Jackson was after or who was paying for the events; however, the marketing consultant for his company stated that he'd quit Two Seas by then. [271][272]

The month of November, 2006 saw Jackson invited the Access Hollywood camera group to the studio in Westmeath in Westmeath, and MSNBC reported that he was working away on another album, which was delivered by will.i.am. (169) On November 15, Jackson momentarily performed "We are in the world" in the World Music Awards in London and also acknowledged that he had received the Diamond Award regarding the offer of

100 million recordings. This was Jackson's final open-air performance in his life. He returned in the U.S. in December 2006 after settling living in Las Vegas, and went to the funeral of James Brown at Augusta, Georgia sometime thereafter in which he delivered his apologies, in which he called James Brown the most significant source of inspiration. [274]

In 2007 Jackson and Sony bought a different music distribution company, Famous Music LLC, which was previously owned by Viacom. The agreement gave him freedom to use songs from Eminem and Beck and many others. [275][276] In a brief interview of the Associated Press in Tokyo, Jackson declared that he was sorry for nothing about his career, regardless of any challenges or "purposeful efforts to hurt himand his family". In March of that year, Jackson visited a US Army base situated in Japan, Camp Zama, to receive more than 3,000 soldiers and their families. [278][279]

In September 2007 Jackson was working on his next album which he didn't complete. [280] To mark the 25th anniversary celebration of Thriller in 2008, Jackson and Sony delivered Thriller 25, which included two singles featuring the remixes: "The Girl Is Mine 2008" and "Want to Start' Something' The Year 2008". To celebrate Jackson's 50th birthday, Sony BMG delivered a collection of his most acclaimed collection of hits, King of Pop, with a variety of tracklists for different regions. [282]

As of 2008 Fortress Investments took steps to get rid of Neverland Ranch the ranch that Jackson used to secure the insurance to cover his advances. Fort provided Jackson's obligations towards Colony Capital LLC. On November 1, Jackson changed the ownership of Neverland Ranch's property over to Sycamore Valley Ranch Company LLC which was a joint venture between Jackson as well as Colony Capital LLC. The deal netted the company 35 million dollars. [285285 Jackson was able to auction off some of his memorabilia that included more than 1,000 items by Julien's Auction House. In the days prior to the main public event, Jackson dropped the bartering following the acquisition of up to $300 million in initial deals from various shows scheduled for

London. [286][264]

The month of March, 2009 amid speculation about his finances and well-being, Jackson declared a progression of shows that would be rebounded, called Then This Is It, at a discussion and question-and-answer session in The O2 Arena. The shows were the first major performances following his HIStory World Tour in 1997. Jackson advised him to quit following the show. The initial agreement included 10 performances in London and then performances at Paris, New York City and Mumbai. Randy Phillips, president, and CEO of AEG Live, anticipated that the first 10 dates would be able to get Jackson the sum of PS50 million. [288 It was announced that the London residency was extended to 50 dates following record-breaking ticket deals. North of 1,000,000 tickets were purchased within two hours. The performances were to run from the 13th of July through March 6 2010. Jackson relocated from Los Angeles, where he trained during the week to prepare the way for the show under the direction choreographer Kenny Ortega, whom he had worked with on his previous visits. The majority of his practices were held in the Staples Center possessed by AEG. [290]

Chapter 9: "Death"

On the 25th of June 2009, less than three weeks prior to The main This Is It show was due to start in London and with the show being sold out Jackson was a victim of heart failure caused through a propofol and benzodiazepine overdose. [291The doctor who treated him was Conrad Murray, his doctor gave Jackson various meds to help in sleeping at his lease-hold mansion situated in Holmby Hills, Los Angeles. The paramedics received an emergency call at 12:22 pm Pacific (or (19:22 UTC) and arrived just three minutes after. [292][293293 Jackson was not breathing , and CPR was administered. [294] Resuscitation endeavors proceeded on the way to Ronald Reagan UCLA Medical Center, and for over an hour after Jackson's appearance there, however, were unsuccessful,[295][296] and Jackson was articulated dead at 2:26 PM Pacific time (21:26 UTC). [297][298]

Jackson was treated with propofol midazolam, and lorazepam;[299] his death was caused due to an overdose of propofol. The news of his death spread quickly on the internet, causing sites to slow down and crash due to user overloaded, [301] and placing a significant stress on administrations as well as websites such as Google,[303AOL Instant Messenger, AOL Instant Messenger, [302AOL Instant Messenger,[302] Twitter and Wikipedia. The overall web traffic increased by anywhere in the between 11% and 20 percent. [304][305(305) MTV and BET broadcast races that were long distances of Jackson's music videos. [306] And Jackson specials were broadcast by TV channels all over the world. [307307 MTV temporarily returned to its original music video format, and broadcast hours of Jackson's music videos and news specials that were live that highlighted the responses of MTV characters as well as other famous personalities. [308]

The dedication of Jackson was displayed 7 July 2009 on the Staples Center in Los Angeles The dedication was inaugurated by an individual family's administration in Forest Lawn's Memorial Park's Hall of Liberty. More than 1.6 million people registered for tickets to the event The 8,750 recipients were randomly selected and were each given two tickets. The ceremony of remembrance was among the most watched events on streaming,[310] with an estimated US audience of 31.1 million[311and an expected global crowd of 2.5 up to three billion. [312]

Mariah Carey, Stevie Wonder, Lionel Richie, Jennifer Hudson and Shaheen Jafargholi were among the performers at the memorial and Smokey Robinson and Queen Latifah delivered tributes. [313313 Al Sharpton got overwhelming applause with cheers after he said to Jackson's kids: "Wasn't nothing peculiar about your dad. It was atypical of the things your dad had to control. However, he was able to do it regardless. "[314Jackson's 11 year-old daughter Paris Katherine, talking openly in a way that was interesting, wept while she attended to the crowd. [315][316 The Rev. Lucious Smith led a closing prayer. The body of Jackson was laid to rest on September 3 2009, in Forest Lawn Memorial Park in Glendale, California. [318]

In August 2009 In August 2009, The Los Angeles County Coroner ruled that Jackson's death was an act of homicide. Law enforcement officials have accused Murray of murder in a compulsory manner on February 8th in 2010. In the latter part of 2011 Murray was judged to be in the rightful position for mandatory manslaughter[322], and was detained without bail in anticipation of the sentencing. [323323 Murray was sentenced to four years of prison. [324]

In 2009, at the American Music Awards, Jackson received four post-mortem grants which included two for his collection of Number Ones, bringing his total number of American Music Awards to 26. [325][326] In the time after his death there were there were more than 16.1 million of his collections was sold within the US and more than the collection was sold to 35 million people throughout the world, which was more than any other craftsman in 2009. [327][328] He became the most famous craftsman, selling 1,000,000 music downloads in just seven days, and 2.6 million music downloads. The thrill ride, the

Number Ones along with The Essential Michael Jackson turned into the most popular index collections that beat every new album. [329The aforementioned Jackson was also the primary artist to create four of the top 20 smash hit albums within a single season in the US. [330]

After the flurry of agreements, in March of 2010, Sony Music marked a agreement of $250 million (identical to $296,696,170 when 2020 comes around) in conjunction with the Jackson home in order to extend the rights of distribution in Jackson's Back Index for not less than 2017. the agreement was expected to expire in the year 2015. It was the largest music contract ever signed by a single craftsman in the history of music. They agreed to provide ten volumes of previously unreleased music and a new collection of their work. [331][333] The agreement was extended in the year 2017. Then, in July was when an Los Angeles court granted Jones $9.4 million of sovereignty-related disputed payments to Off the Wall, Thriller and Bad. In July of 2018, Sony/ATV purchased the domain's stake in EMI for $287.5 million. [335]

The year 2014 was the time that Jackson became the primary craftsman to be featured on the top ten song in the Billboard Hot 100 out of five distinct decades. In the following season, Thriller turned into the first collection to be certified for 30 million copies by the RIAA. Each year following it was guaranteed to be 33x platinum following the time Soundscan added streaming and sound downloads in its collection certifications. [337][nb 3]

The main post mortem Jackson song, "This Is It" written in the 80s along with Paul Anka, was delivered in the month of October. The legendary Jackson siblings reunited to record the backing vocals. The film was followed by a film that told the story of how they went about making the This Is It visit, Michael Jackson's The Is It album, and an album of accumulation. In spite of a limited 14-day commitment, the movie transformed into the highest net-earning show or narrative film to date, earning an estimated revenue of $260 million across the globe. The Jackson home accounted for 95% of money. In the last quarter of 2010 Sony gave the primary after-death album, Michael, and the special single "Letting it be known". Jackson's fellow teammate. i.am expressed his displeasure, saying that Jackson would never have backed the release. [344]

Computer game creator Ubisoft created a music computer game featuring Jackson during the 2010 Christmas season. Michael Jackson: The Experience It was one of the most popular games to use Kinect as well as PlayStation Move, the movement distinct camera frameworks designed for Xbox 360 and PlayStation 3. [345345 Xscape which is a collection comprising previously unreleased music, was released on the 13th of May, 2014. In the following time, Queen recorded a duet that was recorded by Jackson as well as Freddie Mercury in the 1980s. 70] A collection, Scream, was delivered on September 29, 2017. [347]

In October of 2011 the theater company Cirque du Soleil sent off Michael Jackson: The Immortal World Tour, a $57 million production that was staged located in Montreal which was followed by a seven-year show that is based at Las Vegas. 349] A larger and more exciting Cirque production, Michael Jackson: One was planned for a permanent stay in The Mandalay Bay hotel in Las Vegas it opened the 23rd of May, 2013 in a renovated theater. A jukebox melodic, MJ the Musical, premiered at Broadway at the end of 2022. [352]

In April 2011 Mohamed Al-Fayed, executive of Fulham Football Club, divulged the statue of Jackson in the arena of the club, Craven Cottage. The sculpture was transferred in the National Football Museum in Manchester in May 2014, and then removed from the exhibit in March 2019, following the reintroduction of accusations of rape. [355]

In 2012, as a way to settle a family dispute that Jackson's sister Jermaine took his place on an open letter, slamming the agents who handled Jackson's bequest as well as his mother's advisors over the legitimacy of his brother's will. [356The bequest of T.J. Jackson, child of Tito Jackson, was given the responsibility of co-guardianship for Michael Jackson's children due to false claims that claimed Katherine Jackson going missing.

357] A duet with Justin Timberlake Jackson as well as Justin Timberlake named "Love Never felt so Good" was released in 2014 which made Jackson the most prominent musician to be featured on a top 10 track at the top of the US Billboard Hot 100 every five years. The single was released in 2014 and the single reached the top spot at 9. In November 2019 it was revealed that the production of a Jackson biopic, written by Bohemian Rhapsody (2018) maker Graham King, was underway and the screenplay was written by John Logan. Jackson's home gave King access to Jackson's music and to collaborate alongside King. [359]

In 2013 choreographer Wade Robson recorded a claim declaring that Jackson was physically abused by his body for a long period of time, beginning at the age of seven years old (1989-1996). In 2014 an incident was reported by James Safechuck, who alleged sexual abuse that lasted for more than a 4-year period starting at the age of 10 (1988-1992). Both of them had affirmed without reservation during the 1993 trial; Robson did so again in 2005. in 2015, Robson's case against Jackson's bequest was disallowed because it was recorded beyond an point where there is no possibility of returning. Safechuck's case was also barred from time. In 2017 it was determined that Jackson's relationships could not be considered to be liable for his alleged past actions. The decision was taken into consideration, and on the 20th of October 20th the 20th of October, 2020, Safechuck's claim against Jackson's companies was exempted by the managing judge ruling the case was not supported by evidence that Safechuck was in contact with Jackson's businesses. On April 26 2021, Robson's claim was dismissed because of the lack of evidence to support the claim that the litigants exercised control over Jackson. [372]

Robson and Safechuck played the role of a couple in real details in the narrative Leaving Neverland, delivered in March 2019. Radio stations across New Zealand, Canada, the UK and the Netherlands removed Jackson's music off their radio playlists. Jackson's family condemned the film as the result of a "public lynching",[377 in addition, the Jackson bequest issued an announcement in which they said that the film was being a "newspaper character death in which Jackson endured through his daily life and is currently in the process of dying". Close friends of Jackson such as Corey Feldman, Aaron Carter, Brett Barnes, and Macaulay Culkin, claimed that Jackson was not a threat to the group. Rebuttal narratives, such as Square One: Michael Jackson, Neverland Firsthand: Investigating the Michael Jackson Documentary as well as Michael Jackson: Chase the Truth presented data that disputed the assertions. Jackson's collection agreements were expanded after the documentary. [385385 Billboard director of sales Gail Mitchell said she and an associate met with about thirty music industry leaders who believed Jackson's legacy and could withstand the debate. In the last quarter of 2019 a small number of New Zealand and Canadian radio broadcasts added Jackson's music back to their playlists. They referred to "positive outcomes of the audience overview". [387][388]

On February 21 2019 the Jackson family filed a lawsuit against HBO for breaching an exclusion clause from the 1992 agreement. The lawsuit sought to compel HBO to participate in a secret intervention which could lead to $100 at most a million of damage being compensated for the family. [389389 HBO claimed they did not violate the terms of an agreement, and they also claimed to be as an opponent in their SLAPP protest against the domain. In September of this year Judge George H. Wu denied HBO's motion to exempt the matter, allowing to arbitrate the Jackson will to decide the matter. [390The court ruled that HBO continued to pursue the case, but in December of 2020, the appeals court agreed with the ruling of Judge Wu. [391]

CHAPTER FOUR

Legacy

Jackson has been referred to by his nickname of the "Lord of Pop" for his contribution to changing the way music recordings were recorded and also preparing for the current pop music. Through the majority of Jackson's career, he made an unrivalled impact on the younger generation. His influence spanned beyond the realm of music and influenced the fashion industry, influenced dance and raised issues in global affairs. [392] Jackson's music as well as recordings helped to cultivate diversity of race within MTV's programs and guided the focus of the channel between popular music and R&B and shaped it into an model which was durable. In his melodies like "Man In the Mirror", "Dark or White", Heal the World, "Earth Song" and "They Don't Care About Us" His music was a strong proponent of the environmentalism and racial mixing and challenged injustice. [393][394] Jackson is regarded as the most successful entertainer of all Time according to Guinness World Records. [395][396] He is seen as possibly the most significant cultural symbol of the 20th century. His dedication to dance, music, and design, along with his personal life that was plugged has made him a global persona in the mainstream of society for a period of nearly four years. [398][399][400]

The idea of trying to replicate Michael Jackson's influence on pop stars who were following him is similar to trying to track the effects of gravity and oxygen. The magnitude, the sweeping, and especially in the wake of Thriller's enormous and to the present unrivaled commercial success that there wasn't many crafters who didn't attempt to duplicate a part or a portion of Jackson formulae.

-- J. Edward Keyes of Rolling Stone[401[401

Danyel Smith, a main substantive official of Vibe Media Group and the head of the supervisory team at Vibe who was depicted by Jackson as "the Most Famous Star". [402402 Steve Huey of AllMusic referred to Jackson as "a constant juggernaut who had an array of talents to control the graphs seemingly in a way: a instantly recognizable voice, eye-catching dance moves, awe-inspiring musical flexibility, and a plethora of superstar power". 10. BET declared that Jackson is "essentially the most effective performer in history" with a "sound and style, as well as his development and inheritance keep invigorating professionals of all kinds". [403]

When 1984 began, Time popular pundit Jay Cocks made the statement the following lyrics "Jackson is the most amazing ever since the Beatles. He's the hottest single feature ever since Elvis Presley. He could be the most famous dark singer ever." He played Jackson as the "star of radio, records and rock video. One-man salvage team to help the music industry. A Lyricist who sets the pace for the past 10 years. A singer with the most elegant foot in town. A singer who transcends the boundaries of style and taste, and also a wide range of styles. "[91 in 2003 The Daily Telegraph essayist Tom Utley depicted Jackson as "critical" and an "genius". In Jackson's remembrance in July 7th, 2009 Motown writer Berry Gordy referred to Jackson as "the greatest performer to have was ever alive". On June 28 the 28th of June, 2009 in a Baltimore Sun article, Jill Rosen said that Jackson's life's work had a profound impact on fields like dance, sound, design and music recording, as well as famous. [407]

A pop-punk expert Robert Christgau composed that Jackson's music from the 1970s through the mid 1990s displayed "tremendous imagination as well as flexibility and desire" and "virtuoso beats, drums actions and the vocals (however it was not verses)" and music that "will remain forever as an indictment of the rigid notion that pop music is either smooth or shallow and its end". As the 1990s progressed, and Jackson did not keep an eye on the tumultuousness of his "upsetting life" and his music remained in the forefront and began to form "a curve that's not of a guarantee fulfilled and outlived, but also of something that is moving towards misfortune A wildly exuberant young who is a superstar surpasses all others before, only to turn in a visible way into a lost oddity". In the decade 2000, Christgau stated: "Jackson's obsession with fame and his bizarre lifestyle, heightened by his astonishment it is so offensive to shake dilettantes , that his status as an extraordinary artist is often overlooked". [409]

Jackson was influenced by artists such as James Brown, Little Richard, Jackie Wilson, Diana Ross, Fred Astaire, Sammy Davis Jr., Gene Kelly,[410] as well as David Ruffin. Little Richard was a major influence on Jackson,[412]. However, Brown was his most notable motivation. Jackson later said that when he was a child his mother would wake him up whenever Brown was on TV. Jackson depicted being "mesmerized". [413]

Jackson's vocal style was influenced through Diana Ross; his utilization of the oooh-addition in the early days was a feature Ross used in a number of her tracks as a member of the Supremes. [414 She was his mother figure and he often watched her practice. He stated that he gained a lot of knowledge by watching her movements and how she sang, and she had encouraged him to believe in himself. [416]

The choreographer David Winters, who met Jackson when he was arranging his 1971 Diana Ross TV exceptional Diana! He stated that Jackson was a fan of the beautiful West Side Story consistently, and it was his top film. He honored the film by incorporating it into "Beat It" and in the "Awful" music video.

Jackson was a singer from the age of adolescence and then over time, his vocal tone and voice changed. Between the years 1971 to 1975 his vocal range changed from the soprano of a kid to high Tenor. The singer was renowned for his range of vocals. When he appeared on the stage Of Off the Wall in the final part of the 1970s, the talents of Jackson in the arena of entertainment were well-known; Rolling Stone contrasted his vocals against the "winded incredible flanger" that was Stevie Wonder, and composed that "Jackson's soft, wooded tenor is exceptional. It effortlessly transitions into a stunning falsetto that is used with great swagger. "[422By the time the 1982's Thriller, Rolling Stone composed that Jackson was singing with an "completely mature singing voice" which was "touched by sorrow". [423]

The 1990s' turn saw the debut of the intelligent collection Dangerous. The New York Times noticed that on certain tracks "he is breathless and his voice shakes with a sense of dread or sinks to a scream while murmuring resolutely" and that he has the "pathetic sound". As he sang about fraternity, or confidence, the performer returned with "smooth" singing. "[424] Of Invincible," this is the song that rolling Stone composedat the age of 43, Jackson actually performed "flawlessly vocalized mood tracks and pulsating vocal harmony". [425The 425 Joseph Vogel takes note of Jackson's use of non-verbal sound to convey emotions. [426"426" Neil McCormick composed that Jackson's unique style of singing "was distinct and completely unique". [427]

Jackson did not have a proper music preparation and was unable to peruse or write music documents. He was acknowledged for his being a guitar player, console and drums, but did not have the skills to play these instruments. In the process of creating the music, he recorded his thoughts by beatingboxing and imitating instruments vocally. In describing the interaction the artist said: "I'll simply sing the bass line into the device that records. I'll then take the bass lick, and then add the tune's harmonies on top of the bass line, and that will get the song up and running." The engineer Robert Hoffman reviewed that after Jackson was introduced with a tune he'd composed for the moment, Jackson sang each note of every harmony to a guitarist. Hoffman also remembered

Jackson singing strings sequences of action part-by-part into the tape recorder. [428]

Jackson began moving from early as part of the Jackson 5[429] and he mixed dance in a variety of concerts and exhibitions. As per Sanjoy Roy of The Guardian, Jackson would "flick and take his appendages away like switchblades, or emerge from a cyclone and turn into a perfectly poised toe-stand". The moonwalk, taught by Jeffrey Danielwas Jackson's original dance technique and was among the most well-known dance moves dance moves of the 20th century. [430The moonwalk was a dance that Jackson invented. Jackson is believed to be the one who invented the term "moonwalk" and the dance has been renamed in recent times in the form of the "backslide". His other moves utilized the robot, [49the groin along with"repulsive force" as the "repulsive force" in"Smooth Criminal "Smooth criminal" video. [429]

Jackson studied a variety of styles, such as pop, [10][433soul, [10][155] musicality, blues,[433] soul,[434] rockdisco,[435] post-disco dance-pop [436] and new Jack swing.

10. Steve Huey of AllMusic composed the song that Thriller improved the characteristics from Off the Wall; the songs that were rock and dance-oriented were more powerful, while the pop songs and melodies included were milder as well as more soulful. [10] Its tracks incorporated the ditties "The Lady in My Life", "Human instinct", and "The Girl Is Mine",[437][423][438] the funk pieces "Billie Jean" and "Want to Be Startin' Somethin'",[437][423] and the disco set "Child Be Mine" and "P.Y.T. (Youthful Thing)". [438]

Through Off the Wall, Jackson's "jargon of the snorts, screeches, groansand other asides" effectively portrayed his transformation into a mature, Robert Christgau set up in Christgau's Account Guide: Rock Albums of the Seventies (1981). The title track of the collection suggested to the pundit an equivalent to Jackson as well as Stevie Wonder's "weirdo" personality: "Since adolescence, his first contact with reality is in front of an audience , and in the bed. "[439When he released Thriller, Christopher Connelly of Rolling Stone remarked that Jackson encouraged his long-running relationship with the topic of distrustfulness, as well as other obscure images. [423 A.M.'s Stephen Thomas Erlewine noticed this in the tunes "Billie Jean" and "Want to Begin"Something'". [437"Billie Jean "Billie Jean", Jackson portrays a super-fanatic fan who believes that he fathered her child[10as well as in "Want to Start Something" the singer rants against media and tattle. 423 "Beat It" was a scathing critique of group violence, in a homage to West Side Story, and was Jackson's first successful stone get over piece in accordance with Huey. He noticed his "Spine chiller" was the first piece to give Jackson his advantage, based on the theme that was powerful which was a subject which he re-visited in subsequent years. The year 1985 was the time that Jackson collaborated on the cause tune "We are the World" and later, compassionate subjects became a popular subject in his songs and public appearance. [10]

In Bad Jackson's vision of the brutal sweetheart can be evident in the song "Filthy Diana". [444] The song's lead single "I

Just Can't Stop Love for You" will be a standard love song "Man In the Mirror" is a tune of confession and ambition. "Smooth Criminal" is the inspiration for terrifying assault, brutal attack, and possibly murder. The According to AllMusic's Stephen Thomas Erlewine states that Dangerous depicts Jackson as a mind-boggling character. 445 The majority of the album is devoted to the new jack swing featuring songs like "Jam" as well as "Recollect the Time". It was the principal Jackson collection in which social issues became a major issue; "Why You Wanna Trip on Me" for example is a song that fights starvation throughout the globe, AIDS, vagrancy and medicines. Hazardous includes songs with a strong physical charge such as "In the Closet". The title track is a continuation of the subject of the wild love and the impulsive desire. The last section is a collection of contemplative pop-gospel songs like "Will I See You There", "Mend the World" and "Keep the faith". "424" in the track "Gone To Soon", Jackson gives recognition for Ryan White and the predicament of people with AIDS. [446]

History creates a sense of fear. "447" In the brand new Jack swing-funk rock track "Shout" as well as "Newspaper Junkie" and the R&B song "You are Not All Alone", Jackson fights back against the poor form and the disengagement he feels and expresses his displeasure towards the media. "448" In the reflective song "Stranger on the streets of Moscow", Jackson mourns his "transgress"; "Earth Song", "Youth", "Little Susie" and "Grin" are all operatic pop songs. [447][448] On "D.S. ", Jackson assaults legal counselor Thomas W. Sneddon Jr. who had been arraigned against the youngster in both sexual abuse cases. Jackson describes Sneddon as a racist who needs to "get my, whether dead or not". [449Invincible Invincible includes urban soul tracks, such as, "Cry" and "The Lost Children" as well as numbers, such as like "Astounded", "Break of Dawn" as well as "Butterflies" and mixes hip hop, pop along with R&B with pop and R&B in "2000 Watts", "Heartbreaker" and "Invulnerable".

Jackson presented "Spine chiller" which was a 14-minute music video directed with John Landis, in 1983. The film, with a zombie theme "characterized the music of recordings, and broke down racial prejudices" on MTV that had been released two years prior. Prior to Thriller, Jackson attempted to gain inclusion on MTV and MTV, in spite due to the fact Jackson is African American. [453A push coming from CBS Records convinced MTV to start airing "Billie Jean" and then "Beat It" and "Beat It," which led to an extensive partnership with Jackson and helped other dark music experts in getting recognition. The popularity of his work on MTV helped improve the relatively new channel's review ratings as well as the channel's mainline moved towards music and R&B. His performance of Motown 25: Today, Yesterday Today, Forever changed the scope of live stage performances which made it acceptable for artists to perform lip-sync music videos while on the stage. The style of Thriller is replicated in Indian films as well as jails within the Philippines. "Thriller" signified an increase in the size of music videos, and was deemed to be the most impressive music video of all time by Guinness World Records. [217]

The film "Awful's" 19-minute film, choreographed by Martin Scorsese Jackson, the filmmaker used sexual symbols and movement and even slapped his chest as well as his groin, middle and chest. When was asked by Winfrey during the 1993 meeting regarding the reason why he grew in his stomach, the actor replied that it was constrained suddenly through the sound. Time magazine depicted the "Awful" video as "scandalous". It featured Wesley Snipes; Jackson's later videos often featured popular appearance in roles. [458][459] On"Smooth Criminal, "Smooth Criminal" video, Jackson explored different avenues concerning inclining forward at 45 degrees which was past the entertainer's primary area of gravitation. In order to achieve this feat live, Jackson and fashioners fostered an incredible shoe that would lock feet of the performer on the stage, allowing them to tilt to the left. They were granted U.S. Patent 5,255,452 for the shoe. The video of "Let me be" was not officially released in the US and, instead, in 1989 it was commissioned to three Billboard Music Awards [461] and the Golden Lion Award for its embellishments. The video was awarded the Grammy in the category of Best Music Video, Short Form. [63]

He won his MTV Video Vanguard Award in 1988. In 2001, the award was named in his honour. [462"Dark Or White," the "Dark or White" video was released on the 14th of November 1991 in 27 countries with an anticipated audience of 500 million people that was the largest crowd ever for a single music video in the time. [170] Alongside Jackson It also featured Macaulay Culkin Peggy Lipton, and George Wendt. It was an experiment in transforming music videos. The video was controversial regarding scenes where Jackson is seen rubbing his stomach, vandalizes cars and throws a garbage bin at a client's façade. He apologized and ended the final scene in the video. [159]

"In the Closet" featured Naomi Campbell in a romance dancing with Jackson. [464"Recall the Time "Recall the Moment" took place in ancient Egypt and featured Eddie Murphy, Iman, and Magic Johnson. [465] The music video for "Shout" composed and directed by Mark Romanek and creation creator Tom Foden, acquired a record-breaking of 11 MTV Video Music Award Nominations and was awarded "Best dance Video", "Best Choreography" and "Best Artist Direction". The tune and the video is Jackson's response to being blamed for a kid's attack in 1993. In 1994, a year after the incident, it was awarded the Grammy in the category of Best Music Video, Short Form. It is regarded as the most expensive music video ever made, with a price of $7 million. Romanek has disputed this. 469"Earth Song," the "Earth song" video was chosen to win the Grammy Award for Best Music Video, Short Form. [470]

Michael Jackson's Ghosts is a short film written by Jackson and Stephen King and coordinated by Stan Winston, debuted at the 1996 Cannes Film Festival. It was a little over 38 minutes it was the Guinness world record for the longest music video up to 2013 after which it was eclipsed by the video that featured the Pharrell Williams song "Happy". The 2001 music video of "You Rock My World" lasts for over 13 minutes and was directed through Paul Hunter, and elements Chris Tucker and Marlon Brando. [472] The video won an NAACP Image Award for Outstanding Music Video in 2002. [473]

In December 2009 In December 2009, the Library of Congress chose "Thrill ride" as the primary music video to be protected within the National Film Registry, as an example of "getting across the importance to American society". [474][475The music video was a work of Huey composed the song. Jackson transformed his music film into an art form, a fine art piece and a time-limited device using complex storylines and dance schedules, as well as embellishments and iconic appearances, all as well as separating the racial divide. [10]

Jackson's estimated deals of north of 400 million worldwide records[476][Note 2] makes him among the top selling musicians in the history of music. In all, he had 13 number one songs in the US during his career as a performer more than any other craftsman of the Hot 100 era. [478 The RIAA believes that he is the top-selling music maker ever. Seven times, he was acknowledged and appreciated by the president of the United States at the White House numerous times. The year 1984 was the first time he was honored as a recipient of an "Official Public Safety Commendation" award from Ronald Reagan for his philanthropic efforts. He was honored in 1990 when he was regarded by the title of "Craftsman of the Decade" by George H. W. Bush. In 1992, Bush was considered an "Place of Light Ambassador" by Bush to welcome troubled kids at the Neverland Ranch. [481]

He has won numerous awards and awards, far more than any other well-known music recording artists. His accolades include the 39 Guinness World Records, including the most successful entertainer of all time, [395][396 13 Grammy Awards, [483] and the Grammy Legend Award [484 as well as the Lifetime Achievement Grammy Award.and a record-breaking 26 American Music Awards, including the "Craftsman of the Century" and "Craftsman of the 1980s".

In addition, he won an award from the World Music Awards' Best-Selling Pop Male Artist of the Millennium and the Bambi Pop Artist of the Millennium Award. 486 Jackson was inducted into the Hollywood Walk of Fame in 1980 as an individual of The Jacksons, and later the following year to be an independently-owned craftsman. He was admitted to The Rock and Roll Hall of Fame as well as the Vocal Group Hall of Fame as an individual from The Jackson 5 out of 1997 and 1999 separately and independently as a craftsman. Then, in 2002, he joined in 2002 to the Songwriters Hall of Fame. In 2010, he was the first craftman of the recording industry to be selected into the Hall of Dance Fame and in 2014 the post-mortem was admitted to the Rhythm and Blues Music Hall of Fame. The year 2021 was the time he was one of the first inductees to the Black Music and Entertainment Walk of Fame. [492]

The year 1988 was the time that Fisk University regarded him as an honorary Doctorate in Humane Letters. The year 1992 was the time he received the title to the rank of a nominal lord in Sanwi the customary kingdom located in the southeast of the Ivory Coast. In July 2009 the Lunar Republic Society named a pit in the Moon in honor of Jackson. In August, to mark the event that could was Jackson's anniversary, Google devoted their Google Doodle to Jackson. In 2014 The British Council of Cultural Relations declared Jackson's life to be among the top 80 significant social images of the 20th century. [497The World Vitiligo Day has been celebrated on the 25th of June in Jackson's honor. death, in order to bring the issue to light regarding the auto-invulnerable condition that Jackson was suffering from. [498]

www.ingramcontent.com/pod-product-compliance
Lightning Source LLC
Chambersburg PA
CBHW050406120526
44590CB00015B/1847